PROBLEMS AND PROGRESS IN HUMAN DEVELOPMENT
General Editor: J. H. KAHN

MARRIAGE COUNSELLING IN THE COMMUNITY

MARRIAGE COUNSELLING IN THE COMMUNITY

W. L. Herbert M.A.(OXON) and F. V. Jarvis D.P.A.(LOND)

1966

PERGAMON PRESS

OXFORD · LONDON · EDINBURGH · NEW YORK
TORONTO · SYDNEY · PARIS · BRAUNSCHWEIG

PERGAMON PRESS LTD.,
Headington Hill Hall, Oxford
4 & 5 Fitzroy Square, London W.1

PERGAMON PRESS (SCOTLAND) LTD.,
2 & 3 Teviot Place, Edinburgh 1

PERGAMON PRESS INC.,
Maxwell House, Fairview Park, Elmsford, New York 10523

PERGAMON OF CANADA LTD.,
207 Queen's Quay West, Toronto 1

PERGAMON PRESS (AUST.) PTY. LTD.,
19a Boundary Street, Rushcutters Bay, N.S.W. 2011, Australia

PERGAMON PRESS S.A.R.L.,
24 rue des Écoles, Paris 5[e]

VIEWEG & SOHN GMBH,
Burgplatz 1, Braunschweig

First edition 1970
Library of Congress Catalog Card No. 70–108931

Printed in Great Britain by
Hazell Watson & Viney Ltd, Aylesbury, Bucks

08 006910 X (flexicover)
08 006911 8 (hard cover)

CONTENTS

Editorial Note	vii
Foreword	ix
Introduction	xi
1. Modern Marriage and the Counsellors	1
2. Looking at Relationships	8
3. Relationships in Marriage	14
4. Counsellor and Client	22
5. Approach to Treatment	27
6. Ideas about Treatment	32
7. The Interview Situation	40
8. Areas of Treatment	51
9. Special Problems	58
10. Community Help and Referral—I	63
11. Community Help and Referral—II	69
Recommended Books for Further Reading	75
Index	77

"PROBLEMS AND PROGRESS IN HUMAN DEVELOPMENT"—AN EDITORIAL NOTE

EVERY book in this series will take up a topic that in the past has been dealt with by a variety of professions, each working independently of the other professions which have a contribution to make. The aim of the series is to find a common language in which workers of different professions can communicate.

The topics that have been selected will come under three headings: Disorders of Function; Critical Stages of Development; and Special Situations.

"Disorders of Function" refers to difficulties in the acquisition of skills and performance, such as speech, reading, bladder and bowel control, and also the various educational and occupational performances. The nature of the difficulties or defects in any of these activities will be affected by constitutional and organic factors, environmental and educational influences, and, amongst the psychological processes, there will be those within the individual as well as the interaction between the individual, his family, and others in the world outside.

"Critical Stages of Development" will include the landmarks in biological growth and maturation, and cultural adaptation. From infancy onwards through childhood each stage carries with it new satisfactions but involves difficulties in transition from a previous stage. Each stage has its separate characteristics concerned with rearing, schooling, and adjustment to cultural expectations. The adult stage has its crises of physical, domestic, and occupational life, as have the stages of the climacteric with its anticipation of a somewhat postponed old age in a lengthening span of life.

"Special Situations" will refer to family reactions to illness or defect in one member, to changing material circumstances, and to events which tend to break up the family unity.

It is not intended that any of the books will provide a definitive or exhaustive study of the chosen topic. Each book is, however, intended to appeal to the growing number of workers in all professions who are called upon to deal with the personal and interpersonal aspects of human needs.

FOREWORD

MARRIAGE counselling techniques derive from principles of social casework, but marriage counselling is based also upon assumptions of its own. It is taken for granted that the marriage has an existence with its own normalities and abnormalities. The abnormalities threaten the marriage, and the object of counselling is to help to deal with them in order to preserve the marriage. It is acknowledged that this may not always be possible, and that there are some marriages in which the structure is so unsound that it would be better for the individuals concerned if the marriage were to break up. Marriage counsellors, notwithstanding, subscribe to a value system in which the marriage itself is held to be worthy of the efforts of professional workers. This value system is different from that in which an individual person is the object of treatment and where the marriage is seen only as a helpful, or hurtful, situation in which the individual finds himself. In this latter approach some schools of therapists and caseworkers would hold that it was a duty to explore the individual's conflictful feelings about the marriage, and, in the course of this, such an individual might come to the conclusion (or be led to it) that the marriage was not worth while. The individual's personal interests are supreme and the marriage is a side issue. Those who undertake marriage counselling have chosen to go beyond the concern for the individual, and they direct their attention to the marital interaction.

This book by W. L. Herbert and F. V. Jarvis follows an earlier publication by these authors (Methuen, 1958), and for the present volume use has been made of knowledge which is contained in recent literature. The authors are probation officers and thus members of a profession which was amongst the first to take up marriage counselling as a specific assignment.

Marriage counselling itself has many dimensions. There is that of the family circumstances including the material resources whose provision, or lack of it, affects married life. Next there is the interaction in terms of personal relationship. Lastly, one should never lose sight of the fact that the physical and mental factors in the individual personality of both partners can have repercussions in the two previous dimensions.

Herbert and Jarvis do not enter into the specialized psychotherapeutic processes which are necessarily limited in their professional application. Their purpose, on the contrary, is to discuss the techniques which can be available to the extensive range of professions which are being called upon to cope with family problems in which marital disorder is a main, or important, factor. Social work departments these days, whether well established or newly constituted, are expected to base their work on maintaining the integrity of the family. The Seebohm Report lays down (perhaps too optimistically) that social workers will be expected to provide "counselling on particularly difficult marital problems". Certainly social workers will not be able to escape the responsibility for trying to find some techniques for dealing with the marital disturbances which have profound effects on the total family life and on the individual members of the family. Teachers, education welfare officers, family practitioners, and clergymen are called upon to deal with these problems. They do not ordinarily have the necessary training.

This book is a theoretical and practical introduction to the subject of marriage counselling for all who work in the service of the community. It is included in the series "Problems and Progress in Human Development" which has the aim of offering clear, interpretative accounts of topics concerning critical stages of development, disturbances of function, or special situations. The study and treatment of marital disorder, as described in this book, could be held to be applicable to any one of these three groups of topics.

J. H. Kahn

INTRODUCTION

We are attempting in this book to outline a method of helping people faced with problems in marital situations. We have called the process marriage counselling, although we are aware that there are objections to this, both because the term counselling is used in other and wider fields, and because the expression is used by the National Marriage Guidance Council for the work their counsellors do. The method we describe is essentially social casework, although this again is subject to a number of definitions. Our aim has been to draw out the common elements in the work of counsellors and caseworkers in the marital field in the belief that a realization of shared concepts and techniques will increase co-operation and mutual understanding, and make a better service possible.

We have gone on to suggest that even a passing acquaintance with the ideas and skills underlying the process of counselling will give support to professional people and others who in the course of their work meet marriages in difficulties and assist them in offering constructive help. If such people wish to undertake counselling in its full sense, then, as we indicate, selection and training are essential.

Within the limited space available we have necessarily restricted ourselves to a discussion of counselling with individuals. It has not (unfortunately) been possible to look at the interesting developments taking place in group work in the marital field, some of which, for example, are arising from groups formed to help the families of men in prison.

It might also have been useful to have discussed more deeply the nature of individual personality: how far it actually consists of relationships and attitudes, and how far changes in these reflect changes in personality. This has an obvious bearing on marital relationships. Such a discussion, however, would have taken us to psychological depths unwarranted by the practical limitations we set ourselves.

Any serious examination of marriage and marriage-type relationships must be based on an extensive exploration of many branches of study and of human experience. We have indicated for each chapter some books which will enable the reader to increase his knowledge and carry his exploration further.

We make no excuse, despite some current pessimism as to the future of marriage, for stating our conviction that it is a form of human association which gives an essential framework to the personality, so helping to create in the children—if the situation is propitious—the co-operative, constructive, loving individual essential to any enduring society. The effects of a satisfactory marriage are self-perpetuating. From it develop the individuals who are likely in their turn to marry happily and create successful families. The progression is a geometric one—the effects widening and extending as they reach succeeding generations. Investment by the community of money, energy, and time in sustaining and improving the quality of marriage and family life will thus be amply repaid.

1. MODERN MARRIAGE AND THE COUNSELLORS

> The American marriage ideal is one of the most . . . difficult marriage forms that the human race has ever attempted, and the casualties are surprisingly few, considering the complexities of the task. But . . . it is definitely an area . . . in which a very rigorous re-examination of the relationship between ideals and practice is called for.

Although Margaret Mead wrote this about American marriage it applies to marriage in Western society as a whole. Certainly there is no lack of people willing to attempt such a reappraisal. They attempt it from such a variety of angles that it is not always easy to find common ground. One school of thought is antagonistic to the very institution of marriage. There are those who are critical of its monogamous aspect, and others who question the value or even the possibility of a permanent relationship which can bring satisfaction. The former idea implies permitting promiscuity in relationships between men and women, suggesting that an exclusive pairing limits self-expression and requires too much sexual self-control. Exclusiveness of the relationship is accepted by the latter, but it is urged that permanence is inconsistent with human needs and happiness, since the individual's emotional and sexual satisfaction demands constantly changing relationships throughout his life.

Such views appear to emphasize the satisfactions of the partners, especially sexually, rather than the well-being of any children of the union. Undoubtedly, the protagonists of such ideas would deny that the begetting and rearing of children is the principal object of marriage, and some would deny that marriage in its present form is really a good framework in which the best interests of children can be developed.

Some observers prophesy a fairly rapid decline in the family as we know it, based on conjugal ties. These people see the old patriarchal extended family as having been stable, enduring, and secure, but too rigid to cope with modern demands. The present "nuclear" family is described as unstable, transient, and insecure, and ready to break up under the stress of modern urbanized, industrial, and permissive patterns which are now emerging not only in the West, but elsewhere also. Ease of communication is producing a shrinking world: social and geographical mobility are essential, and will contribute to this family break-up. The signs are clear, it is said—the rising divorce rate, increasing acceptance of extramarital sexual relationships, varied and numerous problems with children and young people, and many more cases of mental illness.

It is argued that marriage also suffers from the high expectation of it. Partners demand more from it than regulated sexual relations, socially approved procreation, and some security for the wife and children. They expect the satisfying of all the needs for affection, companionship, and support once met by a variety of figures within the extended family. If all these needs are not met, disillusion and disappointment set in, and ultimately there arises a desire to break the marriage tie in order to seek again the meeting of satisfactions which are really ideals.

The emergence of women as the equal of men in every field of activity places further strain on marriage. In contrast to the old father-authority pattern, the modern "democratic" marriage, with both partners equally involved in decisions and responsibility, is more difficult to operate and sustain at a consistent level. The capacity to compromise, and to give and take, is essential, and this demands a maturity of personality of considerable quality. Furthermore, the right of women to enjoy a life of social and sexual satisfaction is now accepted as being similar to that of men. This means that now two partners have to experience such satisfaction where formerly only one was considered, so that additional strains will arise when the needs of each clash. Such a problem may arise in the practical field of work, where the wife seeks a career of her own. This situation is developed frequently in plays, novels, films, and television, with discussion but no real solution. Is there a *via media* between the wife who sacrifices everything for her career and the wife who sacrifices everything for her family?

Another argument which questions the stability of marriage points to the changing roles of husbands and wives. The husband may not be the important breadwinner and provider which he formerly was, and materially it is often true that the departure of a father is of less material consequence than that of the mother since the State will come more readily to her assistance. Moreover, the husband has become increasingly involved with domestic tasks once exclusively carried out by the wife. This interchange of roles may be an enriching experience, but it necessitates much adjustment and mutual tolerance. Again, it can cause confusion in the minds of the children as to the precise role of each parent. In later life this may lead to a lack of clear sexual identity. This may be especially true of marriages—and they occasionally exist—in which the wife is the breadwinner, the husband the housekeeper.

Religion has always been the matrix of marriage, but the Christian Church in the Western world has lost much of its authority over the marriage ideal, and this has obviously affected individual marriages profoundly. In the Encyclical "Of Human Life" Pope Paul VI sees marriage as "the wise institution of the Creator to realize in man His design of love", and married love as "faithful and exclusive until death . . . a fidelity sometimes difficult, but always possible, noble, and meritorious". He believes that it is "ordained toward the begetting and educating of children . . . the supreme gift of marriage". This view differs from that of the characteristic modern marriage, in which the drive is towards happiness, sexual pleasure, economic convenience, and social enjoyment of perhaps mundane pursuits.

The Pope's view of marriage is, of course, an ideal to be aimed at rather than a pattern to be achieved, and the document prepared by the bishops of the Church of England under the title *Putting Asunder* accepts considerable modification of such ideals. But all too frequently the aim of the partners in marriage is not towards any specific ideal at all, and frequently there is no clear aim. Each individual partner may have some idea, perhaps confused, of the purpose and place of marriage, but where there is no ideal common to both there is likely to be confusion, if not conflict.

It may also be true that the influx of immigrants into our society, with differing cultures, customs, and attitudes towards marriage, has produced some effect. With some, the marriage tie itself is less strong than ours has been: others have brought with them the concept of polygamy. Apart from these extreme differences, the roles played by the sexes in these many differing cultures vary considerably. Intermarriage must add to the confusion of expectation in marriage which men and women have of each other.

The age at which people marry is decreasing, and the Latey Committee recognized this in its recommendations about the age of consent to marriage. Husbands and wives in their teens may not be young by the standards of some other cultures, but in this culture, where education and training for employment are increasingly intensive and prolonged, such partners may find difficulty in earning an adequate living or finding suitable accommodation away from parents. Although it seems to be established that physical maturation occurs earlier now, emotionally full development is often not realized until the early twenties. The possibility of "uneven" development in the partners in a young marriage is much greater than in cases where the spouses are more likely to be mature; when such development occurs it places great strain on marriages of young people.

At the other end of the scale, the increased expectation of life means that couples are likely to have to live together for much longer periods with the marriage unbroken by death than was formerly the case. There is thus the new phenomenon of life beginning at 40, with the couple thrown more closely together at a time when their emotional satisfactions are no longer so diffused among the children, but must be met increasingly by each other. This may have its own very real stress. It may also mean greater working-out of emotions upon the grandchildren.

There is also the new problem of leisure and the demand for almost continuous entertainment, which can breed discontent when coupled with a marriage ideal centring on the home. Especially is this true when the children are born, and the necessity arises of looking after them instead of going out for enjoyment. With couples who have not reached something approaching a mature adjustment this often brings out dissatisfactions and demands adversely affecting the marriage.

It is possible to go on enumerating the social, religious, and other pressures which are causing the institution of marriage to be questioned. There have been earlier times in which a similar pattern of difficulty was experienced: for example, during the so-called Industrial Revolution of the eighteenth and nineteenth centuries, when population growth and movement, industrialization, and the development of large urban communities brought not only wealth but poverty, hunger, squalor, and disease.

On the other hand, the truth may be that we are moving into a form of society in which adequate and satisfactory marriage and family life is possible for a greater number of people than ever before. Certainly, marriage has never been so popular. There are more married people in our society than ever before, and perhaps greater opportunities for a satisfying life for individuals.

From the point of view of the State, marriage and the family which results from it form an essential stabilizing and socializing element. But no one gets married because the State wants them to. People marry because there is a deep need in them which urges their coming together. Sometimes the relationship is not a married one: merely a condition of living together, or sometimes a homosexual association. Nevertheless, the majority of people seem to need the satisfactions of a regulated heterosexual union which spells safety, security, and social approval. Modern psychology has discovered the value of the family, and sees the emotional atmosphere within the family group in which the child is reared as fundamental to his satisfactory functioning throughout his life.

So much questioning and criticism of marriage, and yet so much expected from it: this is the situation in which the modern marriage counsellor must work. He is the creation of modern society. He has a fundamental and a growing part to play in sustaining marriage and improving the quality of family life. He must learn his craft, develop his skills: but to support him he needs a sub-stratum of professional people who meet marriages in difficulties and who, while not trained counsellors themselves, are nevertheless sympathetic to his work and understand its aims and methods.

At present there are professional social workers distributed amongst a patchwork of social agencies, some of them peripherally concerned with marriage and family problems, and others directly concerned with marriage counselling. Some—but by no means a majority—of these are trained to some extent in marital work in the fullest sense. Alongside them are the trained voluntary workers of the National Marriage Guidance Council, deployed throughout the country though fewer in number than one would like to see. One of our aims in this book is to try to outline the skills of counselling common to these disparate groups, so that both the social worker and the marriage counsellor may be helped to greater understanding of each other's work. Another aim is to try to help professional groups such as doctors, lawyers, and clergy to see how and when prompt and effective referral to a helping agency may be made. Their interest and informed understanding of marital problems in such groups is vital to their solution.

It is possible, if the Seebohm Report is implemented, that local authority social work departments will be set up in which marital work will be carried out, perhaps as a specialist function supplementing the ordinary social work process. This is for the future, and even then co-operation and consultation between specialists in different fields will still be essential, and it may be that this book will play a small part towards creating the atmosphere in which this can happen.

List of Recommended Books

Male and Female, Mead, Pelican, 1962.
Putting Asunder, S.P.C.K., 1966
Of Human Life, Pope Paul VI, 1968.
Marital Breakdown, Dominian, Pelican, 1968.

The Family and Marriage, Fletcher, Penguin, 1962.
Reith Lectures, Leach, B.B.C., 1967.
History of Human Marriage, Westermarck, Macmillan, 1921.
Future of Marriage, Westermarck, Macmillan, 1938.
Essays on the Welfare State, Titmuss, Allen & Unwin, 1958.
Family and Kinship in East London, Young and Willmott, Pelican, 1962.
Family and Class in a London Suburb, Young and Willmott, Routledge & Kegan Paul, 1960.
Report of Committee on Local Authority and Allied Personal Services (Seebohm Report), Cmnd. 3703, H.M.S.O., 1968.
The Tablet (periodical): articles by Jack Dominian in Nos. 6748–6751 (Sept.–Oct. 1969).

2. LOOKING AT RELATIONSHIPS

SINCE this book will be concerned with ideas about people, their feelings and emotions, and how these can be looked at and discussed, it is essential first of all to talk about our view of the basic structure of human personality. This involves putting forward a conception which, although deriving from analytical theory, does not follow rigidly any specific school of thought, but attempts to express what are in our experience the vital issues which repeatedly show themselves. The approach is therefore somewhat pragmatic. There will be few direct quotations from other writers—not because we have not learned a great deal from the writing and teaching of others but because we hope we have been able to utilize such ideas and suggest others of our own. This may seem somewhat arrogant, but in a field where there is so much to learn and so much experiment we believe it to be a justifiable approach.

These opening chapters are concerned with the field of human relationships and especially with their origins in the group (normally the family group); with their fundamental contribution to the development of the individual and especially to his ability to mature emotionally; and with the effects of such relationships and the understanding of them in the field of marriage counselling.

The term relationship as used here involves more than one person or object, and it is concerned with feelings. A simple definition of a relationship between two people is the complex of feeling which exists when they have continuing feelings about one another. The use of the word "continuing" eliminates the brief, isolated, once-for-all contact from which relationship in this sense cannot arise. The feelings involved in a relationship are two-way. Naturally, they vary in depth and intensity and also in content. They may, for example, be loving, kindly, and affectionate, or hostile, aggressive, and destructive. Guilt, jealousy, possessiveness, disgust, anger, and fear are some of the many elements of which they may be composed, and not only is there a confusion of many elements, but also these may vary all the time. At one time quite different feelings may be foremost from another time, within the same relationship.

Relationships also differ in quality. To a great extent this quality varies with the individuals concerned in the relationship, and here the concept of maturity can be introduced. In the same way as the growing person matures physically and intellectually, so does he mature emotionally. This emotional maturity is difficult to define; for most people it is a goal to approach rather than an actual attainment. It involves the capacity to consider the needs of others as well as one's own, the ability to wait for satisfactions and not to demand them at once, to give love and to receive love, and to sustain a continuing and satisfactory association with other people. The maturity of an individual may be judged by the quality of the relationships which he makes, and there is a sense in which we may speak of mature and immature relationships. To speak of relationships differing in quality is to imply a difference in maturity.

In order to illustrate this idea, a scale may be imagined at one end of which is the schizophrenic who is incapable of making a meaningful relationship at all: near to that end also would be the schizoid who is withdrawn and does not communicate effectively. Nearer to the centre would come those who do communicate, but who tend to be over-dependent or over-demanding, dominating or submissive. Moving across towards the other end of the scale, one would find individuals who are able to make more mature relationships in which love is given and received on terms approaching equality, involving mutual respect for each other's personality and mutual consideration for each other's needs. Total maturity in a relationship, as in an individual, is an ideal. There will be elements of immaturity in all relationships, each partner sometimes regarding the other as if he or she were in a parental role, or on occasion being irrationally demanding of love, attention, or submission.

What conditions the capacity of a person to move towards personal emotional maturity and consequently influences his achievement of mature relationships? First of all, there are the latent capacities and the attributes which we bring with us into the world at birth. There is the physical environment in which we grow up; which is more than the house which shelters us and the food which nurtures us, including as it does the wider environment of neighbourhood, school, work, and State. It involves such broad complexities as war or peace, plenty or poverty, industrial prosperity or decline, democracy or dictatorship, employment or unemployment, to mention only a few of the conditions.

More relevant perhaps than these for the marriage counsellor, and perhaps in the personal context even more significant, is the emotional climate into which we were born and in which we grew up. Did our parents want a child? Did they want a son or a daughter, and did we fit into this? Was there affection in the marriage, or tension? Was it a large family, and was there consistent love for each child? Early experience is very wide, is of varying significance, and will affect individuals in quite different ways. Bowlby has shown how, in extreme cases of early maternal deprivation, the personality may be so impaired as to preclude altogether the capacity for making enduring affectionate relationships, and there is an infinite variety of experience even within this extreme situation. There appears to be evidence that those individuals fortunate enough to be reared within an emotional atmosphere of love, approval, security, and reasonable control are likely, given normal physical health and intelligence, to develop an emotional maturity lacking in those whose upbringing is characterized by an unloving and insecure situation.

The child who is loved acquires unconsciously the capacity to give love and to accept it. Because he feels his own emotional needs are met, he is able to develop a consideration for the needs of others. His aggression may be put to constructive use, linked as it is with loving and creative feelings, engendered by an atmosphere of parental approval. He can contribute and share because he is himself emotionally secure. He does not have to control his love-objects or make impossible demands on them for attention and affection as do the emotionally insecure. He finds it possible both to accept and to exercise authority because his relationship with his parents in their authoritative role has been a satisfactory one. If they were mature individuals, he has not in adolescence had to assert his independence by exaggerated rebellion, so that his path to adult status has been that much easier.

It may be assumed that no person has the ideal situation in which to develop, but obviously some people have had a more satisfactory pattern than others. Within the helping relationship which a counsellor hopes will be created in talking with his clients, discussion of early family experiences is encouraged. From this can emerge ideas about the kind of person the client is now, and then—as we shall see later—the counsellor will try to look at ways of offering such insight as may best help in the development of personal understanding. Those clients who are able to accept this may move to seeing the problems of their marriage relationship more objectively.

The belief which gives hope to the counsellor is that all human beings have an innate urge to mature emotionally; that the potential of emotional maturity lies within the infant in the same way as do latent adult physical and intellectual powers. As these latter processes move from infancy through childhood and adolescence to adulthood, so too do emotional processes.

As an infant, the individual feels only his own personal and immediate needs, and he strives to satisfy these through others without any consideration for them. Whether male or female, the child's first love-object is likely to be the mother, and the relationship on his part is a demanding one. Through the stages of childhood, with normal development the love-object changes, and eventually in adolescence is directed to members of the opposite sex and of the same age group outside the family group. This natural process takes place alongside physical and mental development without conscious effort by the individual. He cannot consciously will to become emotionally mature any more than he can affect his height by a conscious effort of will. The drive towards maturity is always there, but where there have been impediments to its expression, a distortion or fixation at infantile or childish levels is shown in what we have designated emotional immaturity. It is part of the counselling technique suggested here that, where necessary and where appropriate, we participate with the client in looking at possibilities of developing more adult patterns of emotional functioning.

It must not be thought that the type of person amenable to remedial marital counselling is normally crippled in any real sense in other aspects of his life. Often he will have positive and constructive achievements in other spheres of activity. The range of immaturity which is here discussed would not normally prevent him from earning a living, pursuing a career, or achieving academic or sporting success, for example. He may, of course, experience difficulties in his relationships with others, but, on the other hand, he may be not only a constructive worker but also a popular member of the various groups within which he moves. The counsellor is concerned with the marriage relationship, and it may be that this is the only one which seems to cause problems. It may, indeed, emerge that this special and very close relationship is, as it were, taking the pressures which cannot be released in other areas of the client's life.

The development of love-objects must also imply the development of hate-objects, and one of the most important elements in the building-up of human personality is the range of these. Those with an insufficiently powerful drive to identify with love-objects, or "good" figures, or in whose infancy few of these existed, will find great difficulty in achieving such emotional maturity as we have been discussing unless given much help. They may develop into the permanently angry people who never really grow up emotionally, or become inadequate to meet the pressures of adult life.

At this stage it is worth emphasizing that the counsellor is not a psychotherapist in the narrow sense. His concern is not mainly with the individual client, but with the marriage relationship. It is possible for two partners, each of whom is emotionally disturbed or have elements of immaturity in their personalities, to build up quite an enduring—and from their viewpoint—satisfactory marriage. It must be accepted that although the counsellor will frequently be concerned with immaturity and insecurity in each partner of the marriage, his main object will be to understand how these react on the other partner (and indeed on the counsellor), so enabling him to assess their importance in the marriage itself.

For many of us our marriage will represent the closest, most intimate, and enduring relationship we shall ever make. If all goes well it can be the source of the greatest well-being, happiness, and reassurance of personal worth. If all is not well, it can result in misery and emotional suffering not only to the couple but to their children and even to their relatives. Where this relationship can be understood and constructively helped, counselling is infinitely worth while.

List of Recommended Books

Human Growth and the Development of Personality, Kahn, 2nd edn., Pergamon, 1968.
The Origins of Love and Hate, Suttie, Pelican, 1960.
Child Care and the Growth of Love, Bowlby, Pelican, 1953.
The Integrity of the Personality, Storr, Pelican, 1964.
Two Short Accounts of Psycho-Analysis, Freud, Pelican, 1966.
Psycho-analytic Studies of the Personality, Fairbairn, Tavistock, 1952.
Our Inner Conflicts, Horney, Routledge & Kegan Paul, 1964.

3. RELATIONSHIPS IN MARRIAGE

OUR personalities, then, are influenced, or, as some would say, conditioned, by our early emotional experiences, and the infant's first experience of loving feelings are those involving its mother. A baby's earliest emotions of hate and anger are also directed towards the mother, since its needs are often overpoweringly compelling, and mother must inevitably sometimes appear to the child as a frustrating and denying figure. The love–hate relationship thus built up for the mother seems to be repeated in varying degrees in later life in relationships involving emotional depths, and certainly within the marriage relationship.

Most of our readers will be familiar to some extent with the concept of the unconscious in considering the personality. Whilst much of our behaviour is directed by the conscious or rational part of our mind, some of it is motivated by emotions of which we are unconscious. Certainly it must be accepted that within a deep relationship there are factors which have helped to create it and bind it together, of which the participants remain unconscious. Such elements are more likely to be those which are unwelcome to the conscious or rational part of the personality. Hatred, for example, is not an easily acceptable emotion, and since marriage is socially regarded as a love relationship, anger and hostility in the partners are likely to be repressed. Nevertheless, they remain part of the relationship, even if they are expressed only occasionally by some outward sign of anger. Some couples are astonished, frightened, and subsequently experience feelings of guilt, at the intensity of anger which they can feel, and which they later try to convince themselves was about "nothing".

It will sometimes be the function of the counsellor to help

one or both partners of a marriage to accept the hate in the relationship as a counterpart of the love, and to realize that the expression of angry, hostile feelings need not necessarily mean the end of the marriage, and indeed, the realization that these feelings can be shown without provoking retaliation may be helpful in lessening the guilty feelings which may result.

There will always be much confusion about the existence of loving and hating feelings, and the ability of each partner to express or accept them. A more difficult concept must also be faced—that the existence of both sets of feeling may occur simultaneously, so that the partner at this time becomes uncertain and confused by these contradictory emotions and becomes puzzled, shocked, and perhaps frightened. He may wonder whether he had any "real" feeling. This question of the "good" parts and the "bad" parts of the personality is one which forms a theme throughout any discussion of marriage relationships.

Arising out of the mother–baby situation also is the element of possessiveness. The infant's feelings for the mother are devouring and possessive, and the recognition that this relationship (regarded as a basically loving one) must be shared with others such as father, or brothers and sisters, may be slow in arriving. It may well be thought to be the beginning of socially acceptable emotional development. Yet the primitive wish to have mother exclusively to oneself, hidden and controlled though it may be, undoubtedly survives, to receive some satisfaction eventually in the apparent exclusiveness of early married love. Some analytical theory goes so far as to suggest that there is an element of guilt about incest in some marriages buried very deep indeed.

Excessive possessiveness of a marriage partner may usually indicate immaturity, although there is an element of it in many marriages. The more mature person will be happy to see this exclusive possessiveness disappear in the extension of loving feelings to others—to children, for example, or to relatives and friends. The less emotionally mature, however, find this sharing of love less easy to tolerate, but wise counselling may help them to come to terms with this carry-over of early primitive feeling which is making the marriage unhappy.

Together with the need for love there exists in most individuals a need to give love. In loving another, consciously or unconsciously, we have the feeling that the good within us outweighs the bad; that we have sufficient love and goodness in ourself to meet our partner's needs as well as our own. Marriage can therefore be an unconscious reassurance of the good we possess. The infant may feel badness and guilt at its hostile feeling for the mother, who although sometimes frustrating, is the means whereby its needs are met and the source of both sustenance and love. This guilt may be carried over into adulthood, but can be lessened in marriage by helping and cherishing one's partner. Marriage therefore may meet yet another primitive and basic need—that of enabling people to make, as it were, reparation for the hate which they feel to be wrong, and through this reparative feeling to reduce their guilt about it.

Since in our society romantic love is generally accepted as a basis for a marriage relationship, it is unusual to look in great detail at anything beyond this when two people get married (or, indeed, live together without marriage). Apart from the frequent "I can't think what he sees in her" (or she in him), it is not always clear why couples choose one another. Here, again, there are unconscious elements influencing choice, and these are connected with parental ties. Some of the more unconscious needs that marriage in general may satisfy have been considered, but there will be others peculiar to the individuals concerned. For example, a woman may be attracted to a confident and apparently dominating male. If she has an unconscious need for the security of an inferior role and the man can sustain a position of superiority and authority—indeed, himself has an unconscious need for a submissive partner—then all may be well. These apparently less mature parts of each personality may be thought of as "fitting" or complementing each other. But conflict may arise if his confident manner is in fact a cover for a deeply felt and unrecognized feeling of inferiority, and in the close intimacy of married life he is unable to play the part which his wife needs him to play. He may not be an effective provider, or, if he is, he may not be strongly potent sexually. In such a case, the unconscious "fit", or the collusion between the unconscious needs of the couple, might not remain in balance and the marriage would suffer.

This is but one example of many situations which, if recognized by the counsellor, may be the subject of effective help. We have already indicated that within all relationships there will be elements of immaturity, and this is certainly true of marriage. The most confident of husbands will sometimes want his wife to adopt a maternal role with him, sometimes even a masterful one in which she, for example, initiates sexual intercourse. In our society it might seem more natural for the wife to accept a paternal and protective attitude from her husband; the less mature elements might perhaps appear when occasionally she wants him to treat her like a little girl, perhaps using baby talk, as is very common in courtship. These tendencies may on occasion result in the complete reversal of roles, and there are some marriages in which the husband performs the feminine role in the house, whilst the wife will go out to work and act as provider.

One of the dangers of a supposedly permanent relationship based too largely upon immature elements in one or other of the personalities is that one of them may develop emotionally in a different way from the other. This is one of the especial dangers in marriages between very young people. A move towards increased maturity in one partner may upset the balance of the marriage. The counsellor must face the possibility that in facilitating the growth of emotional maturity in the partners of a marriage, he may contribute to the upsetting of the balance of maturity, as we can call it, if one of them responds more easily or develops some emotional stability where it was previously lacking. In such a case, he may well feel that the process might have occurred in any event in due course, and that it may be better that it happened whilst he was in some useful relationship with both partners so that the results can be looked at.

It has already been indicated in which ways the growing personality of the individual is influenced by the relationships or the emotional ambience within the family or group in which he grows up. It is not possible to dwell at any length upon all the psychological processes involved; the psychological dynamics of the family constitute a major study. There are, however, some concepts with which the counsellor ought to have some acquaintance, which have not yet been developed here.

One of these suggests the idea of identification: the child to a greater or lesser extent identifies with the personality (or elements in it) of the parents or parent figures, thereby coming to accept or reject their standards or attitudes. Later he may tend to identify similarly with other relatives or teachers, for example, or some other influential figure in his life. This is very important, and it is in this way that we move towards unconscious stereotypes of male and female roles: an inner picture of the way in which husbands and wives, mothers and fathers, and more generally men and women, should behave.

The idea of sexual roles is uniquely individualized, and it is crucial to any attempt at the understanding of marriage counselling. The feelings which a person has about himself or herself as a male or female must be connected with the relationship each person makes with others, and the playing of male or female roles in life as well as in the marriage. The expectation of the rights and duties within the marriage will be based on such identification as well as upon conventional social ideas. A marriage in which each partner has a radically differing conception of the duties, responsibilities, and status of men and women is likely to get into difficulties at some time or another. Moreover, since the concepts will be largely unconscious, each will have a strong conviction of the correctness of his own and the error of his partner's attitudes. The skill of the counsellor must often be directed towards understanding some of these unconscious attitudes and stereotypes, even though he is not trained to deal with them deeply. This is the work of the analyst or psychotherapist.

Another common phenomenon which will certainly be encountered by the counsellor consists of a situation in which one partner will try to disassociate himself or herself from unacceptable feelings, attitudes, and behaviour by attributing them to the other partner or to some other person or group. This is done because he finds them intolerable, and by, as it were, "projecting" them on to someone else, he can condemn them at a safe distance and without involving himself. Again, this whole process is an unconscious one, and therefore difficult for the individual to face or to deal with. A man who is unconsciously worried about the violence of his sexual feelings may be correspondingly violent in his condemnation of the sexual activities of others, and this may be a safe and even socially applauded thing to do. But in such a close relationship as marriage this situation is likely to occur with much frequency, and indeed the theory has been advanced that people marry partners who play into their own feelings of badness in a very positive manner. However this may be, there is no doubt that, especially with less mature couples, anger at their own "bad" feelings unconsciously attributed to the other partner often becomes a significant and bitter factor. Again, the skill of the counsellor will be engaged in trying to look with each of them at the way in which they are behaving towards each other and their lack of understanding of its significance.

The sexual area of marriage, often felt to be the most important of all, really symbolizes every other part of the relationship. In this sense it is of considerable importance. Each partner brings to this physical act not only the biological attributes, but also the whole psychosexual development of the personality at that stage. It will therefore include all the feelings already mentioned, especially those associated with mother-love and hatred; the identification with sexual role; and of what may be called fantasy or vivid half-conscious images. These fantasies may spring from the kind of guilt feelings described earlier, or from those of tenderness and love. They may range between extremes of affection and of fear. The realization of this would perhaps help many people to a clearer understanding of the act of intercourse, which can express the union of two people in its most loving form.

Sexual intercourse should be not the main object of marriage, but a way of communication of the feelings which exist between the couple. If loving feelings preponderate, then there will be a sense of security, and a reassurance that the aggression of the sexual act can be accepted as good and creative. Conversely, where the infantile fantasies of damage and destruction still persist to a serious degree, then marital difficulties will be increased.

There is often a great deal of fear about the whole area of sex, especially in people by whom it is imperfectly understood, or represented as dirty and painful. There can be a feeling that one will be impotent, or frigid, or in some way unsatisfactory sexually, or that one's partner will be demanding or "over-sexed". These feelings will derive from the early ones of rejection or inferiority, and because their roots are largely unconscious, they may be very frightening. It is not enough for the counsellor to enjoin patience and understanding, to explain that some people are more easily aroused to sexual activity than others, and to urge the acceptance of the other's sexual psychology. This is a matter of extreme importance and must be dealt with at length and with all the possible implications being understood by the counsellor. Even in these days of premarital sexual experience, it is surprising how often the first time that the sexual act has been attempted has left a tremendous impression for good or ill, especially on the woman. This is the area of marriage relationship where the emotional is always likely to overwhelm the rational feelings.

Apart from these deeper considerations, there are more practical problems arising which ought to be looked at in any discussion about sex in marriage. Questions of wanting or not-wanting children, for example, however they arise, may be vital in the marriage if the couple are not in some agreement about them; and it is frequently inability to realize the emotions aroused, rather than lack of readiness to discuss them, which is the danger. At present, for example, there is the practical and emotional flashpoint of the use of contraceptive methods which may create a serious problem, but which may have been glossed over in the earlier days of the marriage.

Counsellors will certainly realize the depths of such problems, and must try to look at these rather than at the immediate and probably superficial ones which will at first be brought forward. Sometimes discussion of actual methods of sexual intercourse may be useful, but more often such discussion may be something of a defence against the real issues, and a defence used by both counsellor and clients.

It may seem that too much is demanded of understanding and skill from the counsellor, but, as we shall emphasize, counsellors work at different levels. Their insight and their skills will vary. This does not matter basically, so long as there is a capacity to listen to what the client says and to be aware of his feelings. Words and behaviour are indications of these. The essence of counselling is the recognition and the understanding of those feelings, coupled with the attempt to bring them into the open and look at their effects.

List of Recommended Books

Contributions to Psycho-Analysis, Klein, Hogarth, 1948.
Love, Hate, and Reparation, Klein and Riviere, Hogarth, 1939.
Marital Tensions, Dicks, Routledge & Kegan Paul, 1967.
Social Casework in Marital Problems, F.D.B., Tavistock, 1955.
Sexual Harmony in Marriage, Wallis, Routledge & Kegan Paul, 1964.
Three Essays on the Theory of Sexuality, Freud, Imago, 1949.

4. COUNSELLOR AND CLIENT

So FAR we have discussed the influence of the relationships within the family group upon the children and have proceeded to look at the dynamics of relationships within the marriage. The next consideration is to gain some idea of the interaction of feeling between the counsellor and the client. In fact this will be a continuing theme throughout the remainder of the book as we go on to consider treatment in more detail, but it will first be useful to clarify some simple but fundamental points.

Since any relationship between two people must involve a two-way flow of feeling, the counsellor must be concerned not only with the client's feelings, important though these obviously are, but also with his own feelings towards the client and the marriage. Some of these on both sides will be conscious and others unconscious. The counsellor's aim in this area of counselling, as in most others, is to achieve the greatest possible depth of understanding of what is going on in all aspects of these relationships.

He may be expected to have looked carefully at himself. He ought to know something of his prejudices—not just of his strongly held views, but of those attitudes which, arising from his sex, class, nationality, or education, for example, seem so clearly "right". He cannot rid himself of all his views (nor indeed should he try), and has not necessarily to change his attitudes, but he should have become conscious of them and try to make allowances for them in the interviewing situation. It is of especial importance that he should be aware of any major prejudices involving race, colour, religion, class, or sex. In those who are undertaking this work in a "professional" way, a selection procedure such as that of the National Marriage

Guidance Council ought to eliminate those people who by reason of fixed prejudices or rigid and unalterable views are quite unsuitable for this work, although perhaps useful in other spheres of helping. It is also important that he examines and continues to examine his ideas about marriage and relationships between the sexes. He will obviously have opinions, but he should have sufficient perception to refrain from imposing these upon his client; he will know that it is the client's marriage and not his own that he is dealing with.

Even the trained counsellor brings with him into the interviewing room not only his consciously held opinions and attitudes, but feelings also of which he is unconscious. He may have had the opportunity to try to understand this during his training; and discussion of his cases and his involvement in them, with his more experienced colleagues, in case conferences, or in supervision sessions with his tutor, should increasingly extend his insight. It may be usefully interpolated here that a counsellor's training is never completed; it should be a continuing process. This is presumably true of all professional training in the modern world.

The client similarly brings to the interview and into his relationship with the counsellor both conscious and unconscious material. The counsellor listens to what he says, and at the same time tries to draw out and to comprehend the underlying feelings, which will be at differing levels of consciousness.

At this point it should be made clear that it is not the function of the counsellor to solve the client's problems for him. He is not an oracle dispensing wisdom, and it is not his business to advise or exhort or persuade. The true position is one of mutual respect and joint endeavour. Counsellor and client sit down as it were side by side, working together, trying jointly to understand the client's marriage and what is going on in it. The problems which are brought out will be looked at together and the client helped towards his own ideas of their solution.

The counsellor must first of all listen. He must listen with respect and with concern. He is not there to criticize or to condemn. He may, indeed, occasionally criticize, for he is only human, but that is not his real function. He tries to accept the client as he is. This acceptance does not necessarily imply approval, but neither does it involve condemnation. An attitude of acceptance helps the counsellor to see the client as he really is, and it helps the client to feel that he is really being understood. It rids the relationship both of moral imperatives and false assurances. It provides an atmosphere in which the client feels safe and able to reveal himself. In facing this reality together with another, he may be able to go on further to look at his attitudes and behaviour in the light of his own critical self-knowledge. This concept of "professional acceptance" will be something we shall return to in a later chapter.

If the counsellor trails with him into the interviewing room his preconceived ideas, his prejudices, and his unconscious feelings, then the client obviously does the same. But he is unlikely to be trained and experienced in trying to become aware of them. Such is the setting, that whatever the age or the demeanour of the counsellor, the client will often see him as a figure of authority, and may react to him in the manner in which he habitually reacts to those in authority. He may be aggressive and hostile, or he may be meek and subservient. In such instances, he does not see the counsellor as he really is, but carries a fantasy picture of him: a picture conditioned by his early experiences, by attitudes of which he is not aware. It is quite common for such distorted impressions to be formed of people at first meeting. The more mature the individual client, the more quickly his fantasy picture moves into accord with the reality, and conversely, the less emotionally mature he is, then the more likely he will be to project this fantasy image on to the person who is interviewing him.

The counsellor meeting such a person does not hasten to explain that he is not the authority figure the client believes; that he is not terrifying, or imperious, or superior; or that he wants to be friendly, helpful, or sympathetic. Words in such a situation are not usually the most effective means of clarification. The counsellor will rather try to show interest and concern; to demonstrate by his manner and attitude that his purpose is not to dictate, condemn, or control, but to work with the client in reaching his own understanding of his situation and his own solutions.

A possible distortion in the client's apprehension of the

counsellor is the tendency to overvalue him. He attributes to him qualities such as wisdom, strength, and courage which he does not necessarily possess. The client knows nothing of the counsellor's real personality, and he is transferring to the counsellor the loving, adulating feelings of childhood originally felt for his parents or other significant figures in his life. In this situation the counsellor does not accept these, but looks at the reasons behind them.

Another aspect of the feelings engendered in the client towards the counsellor is variation in their intensity and more particularly in their quality. The counsellor soon learns that within the relationship not all the feelings are of affection and gratitude. As we saw in the previous chapter the feelings engendered within any relationship, whether or not they are overtly expressed, are an amalgam of the positive and the negative, of love and hate. Consciously, perhaps, the client is appreciative; unconsciously there will be negative feelings. He may show a puzzling ambivalence—this is commoner with the less mature personality—alternately friendly and hostile.

When one considers the fluctuation of feeling within the most successful of marriage relationships, and reflects upon the very rapid switching of feelings characteristic of adolescence, ambivalence within client–counsellor's relationship will not seem so bizarre. At this stage of the counsellor's experience he becomes more concerned about the client who apparently can only show feelings in one direction; more usually he shows only positive feelings and denies any emotion of hostility, hatred, or aggression. This is the type of person who can only bring himself to say good things about others, and the counsellor, recognizing this as a cover for strong aggressive feelings which the client cannot accept, will aim to create an atmosphere of security in which eventually some of these "bad" feelings can be expressed.

The infant often has fantasies about the omnipotence of his wishes. He feels that whatever he wishes happens, and that his aggressive, hating feelings can do real damage. If this idea is accepted, the corollary is that as the individual develops towards maturity he gains a more realistic understanding of the limitations of the effect of his emotions on the physical world.

It will then be understood how the less emotionally mature person carries over unconsciously into adulthood the idea of the considerable power of his intense feelings. If such a person has demonstrated his aggressive feelings in an interview, he may subsequently feel in some way he had harmed the counsellor, and, fantastic as it may seem, may telephone or even call later to reassure himself that the counsellor is still surviving and is unhurt by the destructive feelings unloosed. The client who cannot show any aggressive feelings at all may well be a person who fears so much his hostile feelings and the damage they may do that he is impelled to repress them. This is one conception of the denial of feeling which is extremely important to look at in counselling work.

The kind of feelings that the client can show in the interview are not only important in understanding the individual himself, but helpful to the counsellor in understanding the interplay of feelings within the marriage relationship; subsequent chapters will consider how the counsellor, in co-operation with the client, uses this understanding to help the marriage. We may conclude here by emphasizing again the extra sensitivity and the extra awareness demanded of the counsellor. He is listening not only to the words that are actually spoken but with an inner ear to the feelings behind the words; and at the same time, he is endeavouring to make a relationship within which the client feels secure enough to reveal more of himself and within which he may feel sufficiently encouraged to work with the counsellor in the exploration and understanding of his situation.

List of Recommended Books

Marriage Guidance, Wallis, Routledge & Kegan Paul, 1968.
Theory of Psycho-Analytic Technique, Menninger, Basic Books, New York, 1958.
The Faith of the Counsellors, Halmos, Constable, 1965.
Psychotherapy—the Purchase of Friendship, Schofield, Prentice-Hall, 1964.
Relationship in Casework, Association of P.S.W.s, 1963.

5. APPROACH TO TREATMENT

WE MUST now go on to consider how the counsellor's understanding of relationships is put to use in practice. From what has been said it will be clear that he seldom considers a marital problem in terms simply of material or social difficulty, although these may be elements in the situation. Although he is, of course, interested in each individual partner in the marriage, his central concern is the relationship between them, and his approach to the problem is in terms of this.

He is interested, as we have indicated, in the maturity both of the partners and of their relationship. Resting his hopes upon the human drive towards emotional maturity, a major aim will be to further that maturity. This is a fundamental point. It primarily explains why it is that the counsellor seldom resorts to direct advice. He is dealing with emotions and it is clearly useless to advise a client to develop emotionally. A necessary condition for a move towards greater emotional maturity in the client is first an understanding of his own attitudes and behaviour as they are at present, and it is this that the counsellor attempts to facilitate.

There are various levels of approach to a marital problem and it is useful to look at these critically. At the lowest level there is the ordinary kind of discussion which is normal between friends of the couple who may be asked to intervene, and this is all too often the level of many professional people who should know better. It consists of directing the problems away from the marriage and towards the superficial emotion; for example, the couple may be urged not to part for the sake of the children. It may be said that they should stay together because of the scandal which separation would cause, or there may be a strong appeal to moral or social values which they are flouting. This kind of "help" is apt to do more harm than good, because there is no attempt to get at the underlying difficulties, and even if the situation is temporarily patched up, it will almost inevitably recur in a much more intractable form, or the couple will stay together in a state of hidden hatred which is often a far worse situation.

The next level is that of attempts at advice or reassurance. This kind of approach attempts to solve the problems by means of directive advice. It may consist of trying to sort out the housekeeping money to best advantage, or looking at the couple's tendency to quarrel because the husband goes out too much without the wife, and suggesting remedies for this without realizing the underlying reasons for the problem. This kind of practical consideration, of course, is frequently present, and is usually the first thing which the client will raise. Certainly at some stage it must be talked about, but the difference between the reassurance of the advising welfare worker and the search of the counsellor together with the client for deeper causes is simply the difference between dealing with effects and dealing with causes—between cutting off weeds and searching out their roots.

Counselling, in the technical sense in which we have used it, is the third level of approach. As we have seen, it consists of a patient building up of a relationship in which the client can look more easily at the way in which he is bringing his emotions into the marriage, how he is using these in this special relationship, and how and where they conflict or collude with the feelings of the spouse. The interplay of these feelings is the real field for the counsellor.

At another level still is the use of psychotherapy, which needs special skills and is normally directed to one individual and will not usually be extended to interpersonal relationships.

Finally, psychoanalysis of all approaches is directed most towards one individual. This is, of course, employable only by highly skilled analysts and would seem to be limited also in its application by the ability of the client to accept the special demands which analysis makes.

Having distinguished counselling from other forms of approach, we can now consider its application. We shall be discussing interviewing techniques in greater detail later. Here it is only necessary to note that while much counselling takes place in the normal office interviewing situation, it is not tied to this alone, and effective work may be undertaken in informal situations.

Exhortation and advice have no real part in counselling, as we have seen, but this does not mean that the counsellor has no concern with conscious material. This is far from the case. In fact much of the counselling process will consist of communication on a conscious level. The counsellor listens carefully to what his client is telling him. As he listens he is sorting the material through, relating in his mind what the client is telling him to what he has said earlier. When the counsellor speaks it may be simply to reassure the client that he is listening and is concerned. At intervals he will find it helpful to draw together what his client has told him so far, clarifying the issues and linking them in a way which can be understood. The client will often be disturbed and excited, and his account of his situation and of events may be confused or even contradictory. It can be helpful to him for the issues to be thus clarified, and the choices open to him identified. The counsellor must be careful, however, not to state the situation as he sees it in over-simplified or over-definite terms. As we have said, the process is something akin to a joint exploration, and he will usually preface his clarifying remarks with phrases such as "Perhaps what we're saying is this . . ." or "I wonder if we look at it like this we'll see things more clearly . . .". The exact terms do not matter. It is the tentative, exploratory approach which is important.

Once a helping relationship is established, the counsellor may use it simply to enable the client to feel safe in revealing himself and in looking at his situation. It is sometimes helpful, however, for the counsellor to play a specific role. We must accept that the client will sometimes see the counsellor—whatever his actual age—in a parental role, and many counsellors find it simple, even natural, to appear as the good parent: sympathetic, understanding, helpful, and uncritical. There is nothing wrong with this, and it may frequently be what the client's needs demand, but it is necessary for the counsellor to know what he is doing. He must be aware of the role he is playing and its relation to his client.

Some situations require a special form of parental role. For example, a woman who is inhibited sexually to such a degree that she gains no pleasure from the sexual act may have been brought up by a mother to whom sexual matters were abhorrent and who could give no approval to her daughter's femininity and adolescent sexual development. Such a woman may be considerably helped if a woman counsellor can play the role of the permissive mother, enabling her to talk about her fears and fantasies regarding sex.

The woman client who is depressed, drably dressed, and utterly lacking in confidence and pride in herself may be married to a man who perhaps unconsciously has reduced her to this plight by his biting, sarcastic, critical tongue. With such a person, the counsellor will take care to express and demonstrate his interest and concern. He may attempt to play a supportive and helpful role, listening carefully to what the client says, accepting her feeling of utter unworthiness and badness, and when she is able to bring into the relationship some good aspect of herself—some effective or constructive action or achievement—he will approve it and give encouragement and praise. She may bring a photograph of her children, a knitted garment she has made, even perhaps a diploma in cookery. She may bring a new, improved self—hair well styled, looking more attractive, and more tidily dressed. However she attempts to display the good aspects of herself, the counsellor responds encouragingly and in so doing hopes to restore to some extent her feelings of worth and to counteract her feelings of overwhelming hopelessness and badness. Such interest and concern can later lead to useful discussion at greater depth, but even if it does not, it can still be of help.

The counsellor must realize he is occupying a role-playing situation, and he must be able to respond positively to his client, sense the need, and convey genuine interest and concern.

We have already seen that both counsellor and client bring into the interview and into their joint relationship much feeling that is unconscious. The counsellor as he grows in experience will become increasingly aware of unconscious motivations in his client. He is not really trained to deal with these as the psychoanalyst is, and will often prefer to leave his understanding unspoken. Sometimes, however, there may be material on the threshold of consciousness, material which seems repressed or blocked, and which, if it could be brought fully into consciousness and understood, would help the client towards new insight and perhaps changed attitudes and behaviour. In such circumstances, the counsellor may attempt to interpret to the client feelings underlying what he has said or what he has done. This is normally a delicate process undertaken cautiously. Perhaps, for example, the client has indicated in a number of ways during the course of one or two interviews that as a child he was jealous of his sister, and he may later on be giving his opinion that women always get preferential treatment in restaurants. The counsellor may at this stage, linking this remark with previous remarks, attempt to show the client his underlying jealousy which in adult life he tends to extend to all women. On another occasion he may go on to suggest to the client that some of his attitudes and behaviour towards his wife stem from these same long-buried but still active, angry, envious feelings towards his sister who seemed so unfairly to get more of his parents' interest and love than did he.

This form of insight-giving is not easy. It demands not only an extra sensitivity and awareness but a delicate sense of timing too. The client will sometimes not accept the interpretation. It may be that he is not ready for it, that it will always be unacceptable, or even that the counsellor's judgement is wrong. Experience will teach the counsellor when and if to renew the interpretation on a later occasion. In general, we suggest that only experienced and trained counsellors should attempt work at this level.

List of Recommended Books

A Modern Approach to Marriage Counselling, Herbert and Jarvis, Methuen, 1958. Reprinted by The Family Life Movement of Australia in 1969.
Marriage for the Married, Macaulay, Delisle, 1964.
Ups and Downs in Married Life, Griffith, Methuen, 1966.

6. IDEAS ABOUT TREATMENT

IN THIS and the following chapters we shall look further at methods of relating these ideas to practice. At the same time it will be possible to indicate an approach whereby, apart from trained marriage counsellors, many who find themselves concerned—sometimes against their will—with problems of the marriages of others may be enabled to offer some support.

"Treatment" is used here in its widest sense. If the preceding chapters have been accepted, the reader will understand that the problems which are encountered can be seen in the context of relationships and not simply in a material or social setting.

We would hope that many of those who have some responsibility for helping others can learn to perceive the existence of deeper problems, even if they do not feel able to deal with them. If such problems can be recognized, then it may be possible to make some assessment as to the need for specialist help. There are cases in which something can be attempted before such help is asked, or even whilst it is pending. If, for instance, an appointment is made with a specialist counsellor, it may be for a long time ahead, and if the person referring can sustain a useful and positive relationship with the client during this waiting period, he may not only assist the client directly, but also prepare him for more expert help by outlining the way in which such help will be given, and also by giving him some reassurance as to its outcome.

Treatment, then, may be a very short-term process of recognition and referral, or it may be a form of on-going relationship in which feelings are brought out and an attempt made to look at them in a therapeutic way. The period during which such relationship is sustained will depend also on the personalities involved and on other factors such as the skill and ability of the individual counsellor, the nature of the problems, and the outside and inside pressures affecting each person involved.

It might first be of some importance to look at the possibility that clients choose either consciously or unconsciously the people from whom they seek help with their problems. Obviously, the person seeking divorce would be expected first to go to a solicitor, and although this is frequently true, it is not always so. In our experience, many who know that probation officers are trained in marital work will often first go to their local probation office, even though they will initially assert that they want a divorce or "separation". Perhaps many of these people come to this source of help because their feeling about the situation is associated with guilt and the need to be punished, however deeply buried such feelings may be. Many such people see the probation officer as an agent of the courts and so connected with law and punishment. Others will go first to their medical practitioner, perhaps seeing or unconsciously realizing the need for reassurance or for a confidential and strictly professional relationship, or believing that the marital difficulty stems from physical troubles.

This is related to the interesting question of the "image" presented by the specific person who may be approached. Many professional people would be surprised at the ideas which their patients or clients have about them and their profession. Social workers who ask a church member seeking their help why she has not been first to see her clergyman are often told "I am much too ashamed to go to him" or "He wouldn't understand—he is not concerned with that part of my life". On the other hand, many people do not realize that there are trained social caseworkers who can help, and often believe that such workers are restricted to dealing with specific problems such as mental illness or difficulties with children. It is always of use to try to assess the reason why a client chooses to talk with a particular person or agency about marital problems and what sort of view she may have of that agency.

It is also important to try to find out why the client has come at that particular moment; why it has become of such urgency just then that help should be sought. Presumably there must have been some crisis, material or physical or psychological, and more usually a combination of all three. As we have seen, the reason immediately given will mask a variety of unconscious motives for coming.

Clients will not often see this "seeking advice" as asking for treatment, and sometimes they will assume that a single talk with the worker will produce a good result. Again, all counsellors are familiar with the client who asks that her husband shall be seen and "given a good talking to", as though the problems, and all that has gone on during years of married life, could be sorted out in a few well-chosen words. If the counsellor believes that it is possible, he will have to discuss this aspect with the client during the first interview or consultation. Much will depend upon the way in which the interview has come about. If it is by direct approach, then there must be certain expectations about the role and function of the counsellor in the mind of the client, however vague or ill defined these may be. A wife may feel that the counsellor is a person of considerable power or knowledge, or that he has some special influence or ability, or she may expect a form of action which is almost magical.

On the other hand, if she has been referred by another agency, she may see this as a rejection. For example, a wife referred to a probation officer by a medical practitioner could feel angry and humiliated, and may not at all understand why this has been necessary. In such cases, the utmost care is needed on the part of both the referring person and the person who accepts the case to explain exactly why one agency is better able than another to cope with her problem.

If the doctor can say that the probation officer or the marriage counsellor is specially trained to deal with such anxieties, then he is giving more effective help to her and to the other worker than if he says, for example, that he has not the time to help her himself but knows someone who might have. Nobody likes to feel that someone else cannot spare time for them, but this is too often given as a reason for referral.

The first interview is a most anxious occasion for the client. She probably will have had to key herself up to talk about some of the deepest difficulties she has ever had to face, and the attitude of the counsellor is of paramount importance. Later in this book we shall talk more about the interview in general and the first interview in particular, but certainly a client may easilv be inhibited from any further contact by what she may feel as an unhelpful or rejecting reception by the person to whom she has come for help and guidance.

Because of the difficulty most people experience in discussing the intimate involvements which arise in the marriage relationship, many will at first express themselves badly, and put forward general ideas of the problem. "All I want is happiness" is a common cry. Others seek security, or affection, or some greater freedom. It is often possible even at this stage to relate such ideas to an overall pattern of the client's life. The client who seeks security will often be the one who has felt deprivation or rejection as a child and who has lived with this feeling ever since.

It is clearly useful to make some sort of working diagnosis as soon as possible, but it is also essential to appreciate that the ideas expressed may have a meaning peculiar to the client, and they must sooner or later be related to the interplay of the feelings in the marriage. Why, for instance, did the wife deprived of affection as a child marry the particular man she did?

From the first interview there must be the acceptance of the client we touched upon in Chapter 4. This acceptance must exist on both sides, and it is not quite so simple as it may appear. In the normal sense, it may denote a willingness to help, but the implications of the term in the technical sense in which it is used here are much deeper. By acceptance we mean the counsellor's attempt to enter into the feelings of the client and to accept both the bad and the good which exist. This is a difficult concept to explain, and it does not mean acceptance in the sense of approval of the *actions* of the client. For example, if the counsellor is confronted by a husband who admits to wife-assault, his first reaction may be one of indignation, or of anger, or of repugnance. Such responses must be controlled since the real effort is to direct attention to the factors within the personality which cause the assault, and to attempt to understand their underlying motivations. It is probable that the husband himself is ashamed of his actions, and is in a state of confusion or even horror at what he has done. To upbraid him would be useless, and so the worker has to try to "feel with" him—to accept the fact that people do bad things as well as good, and perhaps even to accept that this was something the husband did from some perhaps very deep and even unconscious motive.

This idea of acceptance is one of the chief reasons for the widespread though erroneous belief that the counsellor condones and tries to justify any kind of behaviour on the part of his client, however socially or morally reprehensible this may appear. It certainly is very closely bound up with the conception of being non-condemnatory. For those who have very strong moral principles it may seem difficult to accept that whatever evil a man does we should try to understand the individual and his motives with the possibility of looking with him later at the results of such actions, and yet not go on to condemn him. It must be faced that those who are to attempt to work in the field of marital relations must, as far as possible, keep their own scale of values out of their work with their clients. In many cases it is essentially the client's very feelings of being a "bad" person which increases his difficulties. He needs someone to accept them, to acknowledge that they exist, and yet to continue working with him as a person who is worth caring about in spite of them. The achievement of such an accepting relationship is something every worker in this field is striving for all the time. It does not mean the condoning of evil but rather the facing of what seems to be evil-doing together with the person who commits it, in the hope that he can be freed through his own efforts from such behaviour.

Such acceptance of the client, with all his good and bad feelings, clearly involves the counsellor's feelings also. Something of this has already been said. There is a strong school of thought which believes that workers in this situation must at all costs keep their own feelings out of the relationship which they form with their clients, and strive for a "clinical" relationship. This seems an almost impossible conception, and it would seem better to acknowledge that the counsellor has feelings about his client and about his client's situation which may well affect his judgement, and then to try to understand such feelings so as to perceive where they are likely to "get in the way". In this sense, there is a control of the involvement by the counsellor to the extent that he quite honestly recognizes that his emotions and prejudices are likely to come into play in dealing with another person, and that he does his best to allow for this. In a word, he sees himself engaged with another person whom he accepts in a caring way as an individual, in an effort to look at the problems which are presented to him and help the other person towards any possible solution which that person can accept. He recognizes that each has needs and anxieties in the undertaking.

The mention of needs and anxieties is a reminder that ideally the counsellor is there to be used by the client. Such use may well be in the form of fulfilling a particular role which may meet a special need of his client. Sometimes the need may be a very deep one, such as the necessity to share, or even to transfer, a hopeless sense of overwhelming guilt or anxiety. It may sometimes be a more obvious one, such as a need for emotional support and a caring relationship with an accepting person, so that there can in this way be a discussion of the marital problems with the feeling that at least one other person is trying to understand without apportioning blame or guilt.

Bound up with these is a frequent need for affection and its converse the need to be able to show hatred and hostility without being condemned. Hostility for many counsellors is difficult to accept, since most of us in the "helping" professions are apt to see ourselves as meriting respect, if not affection. It may well present a problem which we cannot easily solve when we are confronted by a client who seems only to dislike us and to express dislike in a very definite manner. Yet it is such persons who are in the greatest need of help, since they are often painfully aware that they are in some way intolerable to their fellows. They will test out the counsellor to the fullest extent by displays of anger and hostility. They are really trying to make him into a bad figure so that he can be relegated to the gallery of all those others whom they have known who are unable to accept them. They will make tremendous demands on him and on his time, and will go to the extreme in half-conscious efforts to force him to reject them. If he does reject them he becomes another bad figure and by so much is their state made worse. It will be additional confirmation of their feeling that they are so bad that nobody wants to know them, and their bitterness as displayed in hostility will be increased.

But if the counsellor is able to accept this anger, and slowly show how it has developed and what it means, then it is possible that some better adjustment may be made. The fantasies of guilt may recede with the realization that someone has perceived their origins, and does not condemn. Fear and anxiety may then be expressed, perhaps for the first time, with consequent relief of tension.

Other clients have a deep need for security. Many of these needs are interlocked, and it is clear that love and hate and security in personal relationship are linked. Clients display these varied feelings in different ways, and it is not always easy to recognize them in the confusion of the problem at first presented. A client who needs a secure relationship will often be troubled by superficial fears of breaking appointments or of driving the counsellor away. There is a seeking for consistency and stability from the counsellor which the client may feel she has never before experienced. This may, of course, be a fantasy feeling, but it is a reality to her and must be accepted as such at first.

There are those whose need is for someone to whom they can come in an almost impersonal manner, with whom they can be reflective and talk without having to create an impression of goodness or intellectuality. This is akin to a conception of the counsellor being as it were a mirror to his client. There can be much warmth and security in such a relationship, even if nothing more is attempted.

Other clients, as we indicated in Chapter 4, are greatly helped to understand the problems of their marriage if some effort can be made by the counsellor at interpreting even in a simple way the significant statements they make. For example, a wife who feels that her husband is devoting to their daughter much of the attention which he formerly gave to her may be helped to recognize some of the jealousy which exists on her part towards the daughter. Later on, this may be used as a stage in looking at her much deeper fears of loss of sexuality. Much of the skill and ability of the counsellor lies in recognizing and linking ideas even when they are presented in a different context, and in looking at them with the client in their simpler form. The real reassurance which results is worth the considerable effort involved.

Throughout all this counselling process there runs the vital problem of love and hate relationships. This exists not only between husband and wife, but also between counsellor and client. The idea that love must be a continuous emotion, and that anything akin to hatred is a feeling which must be avoided, is the cause of more guilt and conflict than almost any other. Patient disentangling of the "good" and the "bad" feelings is necessary if anything of a permanent relationship is being established, and this involves the concept of acceptance already mentioned.

List of Recommended Books

The Casework Relationship, Biestek, Allen & Unwin, 1961.
Marriage: Studies in Emotional Growth and Conflict, Pincus and others, Methuen, 1960.
Anxiety and Neurosis, Rycroft, Allen Lane, 1968.

7. THE INTERVIEW SITUATION

We must now turn to some practical considerations with regard to counselling. As soon as a counsellor is face to face with someone with a marital problem, he will have in his mind while he is listening considerations as to how he is to proceed. The true counselling situation as we have described it is one in which the client wants to understand what is happening in his marriage relationship, is willing to explore the situation with the skilled help of the counsellor, and is willing to meet the counsellor at intervals over a period in order to do this. The ideal counselling position is one in which both partners to the marriage accept this point of view.

The counsellor will seldom meet clients spontaneously oriented in this way. Normally he will have to explain his function, identify his role, indicate the sort of help he is able to offer, and outline the demands this is likely to make. He will have to do this while at the same time he is demonstrating a real concern for, and understanding of, the client's misery. Much is therefore demanded of the counsellor during the first contact.

The counsellor's first decision towards the end of the initial interview is to determine whom he should meet next. It was formerly held to be essential that both parties in a matrimonial case should be interviewed as soon as possible, and ideally be seen together. This idea has been considerably modified in recent years, although it is certainly used as one technique in this work. It is now realized that there may be wide variations in technique, always keeping in mind that the concentration must essentially be on the marriage and the personal interplay within it—even when the decision is to continue interviewing only one of the partners.

In the case of a wife, for example, who is confused, uncertain, fearful, and who asks the counsellor not to write to her husband, it will normally be better to arrange a second talk with her to see how far the first has given her any sort of ability to look further into her problems. With a wife, however, who seems a more forceful type (albeit possibly deeply disturbed by guilt feelings), it may be better to approach her husband at once.

The whole question of making contact with the second partner is one which requires careful study. The decision will never be one formulated by rigid rule; it will always be determined not only by the needs of the person who comes first and the situation he presents, but also by the insight of the counsellor in summing up quickly all the factors involved so far as they can be ascertained. Apart from the personality factors, other considerations will arise: the time available, the advisability of contacting the spouse, and the degree of urgency. If there is obvious and continuing violence, it may be necessary to act very quickly, either by seeing the other partner or by referral to the police, or a doctor, or other agency. There may be other urgent needs: for example, a woman who is afraid to return to her husband may have to be helped to find temporary shelter.

An example of a case in which only one partner was seen occurred when a wife was sent by her medical practitioner to a marriage counsellor for help in a situation where her husband was going out with another woman and returning home at night very late and recounting to his wife the sexual pleasures he was experiencing. One might imagine this was an intolerable position for her, yet she did not want to leave him. She said she still cared for him and for the children, who were over school age, but still very vulnerable to emotional shock. The counsellor was able to see her several times, and to take up her feelings of hurt and rejection. In subsequent interviews, they discussed her expectations of marriage. They talked over her realization, which developed only gradually, that the man who had seemed so brilliant and masterful when they married was emotionally very immature even now, and could not resist proving himself sexually potent with women of (he said) much wider experience than his wife. It seemed that this had happened before, but as she grew older she became more and more frightened at the idea of being left alone and unwanted in her forties. The deeper feelings which were revealed included a need for possessiveness of others, and an unusually close identification with a severely crippled father. This produced attendant guilt and conflict about his injury, anger against her mother who left her to look after her father, and, not surprisingly, confusion as to her real position as a wife and mother in her own right. The counsellor could not attempt to solve the basic problems, but enough was done to enable the wife to look at the pattern of her marriage in a much clearer way. She broke off the interviews at a point when she had become able to see herself as a person of value to her husband and children, and to tolerate in some degree his unfaithfulness and cruelty.

On the other hand, in a case where a wife came complaining of violence by her husband against herself and her adolescent children, the counsellor felt it necessary to see the husband as soon as possible. As in many cases of this kind, the wife had married a man of severely delinquent character with the apparent object of reforming him. Her own guilt and desperate need to work out some deep form of reparation became clear in the first interview. When the husband was seen he emerged as a man of lower intelligence and social class, bewildered by his wife's adverse reaction to his attempts at sexual intercourse. When she refused his sexual advances he always reacted violently. This situation was complicated by the fact that it was the wife's second marriage. The children were the product of the first, which had ended in the wife obtaining a divorce because of the husband's cruelty. Only a few interviews were possible here, and the wife decided to take legal action, but before this happened they had both been enabled to see something of the emotions in their marriage, and the way in which each was using the other—in this case principally through the demanding or withholding of sexual intercourse. It was even possible to show them a little of the reasons for such action, the need which each had to use the other in this way, and the underlying fear and anxiety which they both experienced.

There is a variant in counselling technique which has been explored in detail by Dr. Henry Dicks in the "Treatment" section of his book *Marital Tensions*. This consists of the use of two counsellors, one working with each spouse. Our experience has been that this is possible chiefly in an agency where there is a high degree of skill, opportunity for frequent consultation between the workers, and a careful system of preliminary or intake interview before the clients see the counsellors. This system is often used in child guidance clinics. Use is also now being made of this "foursome" approach where two agencies are involved, and it is not now so unusual to find a marital situation being shared, for example, between a probation officer and a child care officer. This type of co-operation will undoubtedly become more widespread as the use of common methods is extended to a larger number of agencies. Collaboration must inevitably increase as agencies acquire greater knowledge of each other's functions, and understand more fully that many of their basic aims and skills are similar, and indeed often interchangeable. This is the basis of the Seebohm approach. On the other hand, there are still considerable areas of work and knowledge in each agency which remain exclusive to it.

Although there is no clear guide to the type of case in which employment of two counsellors is more useful, our experience has been that it is helpful where the emotional demands of one or other spouse are very great, or where one partner is seen to be highly disturbed. Incidentally, it ought to be realized that where there is an obviously disturbed partner, then the other is also likely to present unstable elements in his personality. This may often not be appreciated until after several interviews, but the counsellor should always be aware of it as a probability.

One complicating factor, with both one counsellor and two, is the sharing with each spouse of experience gained in discussion with the other. In a really therapeutic relationship, this is something which may be talked over with each, especially if it is understood that it is the feeling behind what is actually said which is of importance. Undoubtedly, each will be wondering what is passing between the counsellor and the other spouse in interviews. It is well to realize this and to be prepared to look at the feelings involved in it which will be of importance in the marriage. Is the wife anxious, for example, that anything she says is kept secret? If so, the reasons behind this may be taken up.

A difficulty which frequently has to be faced is that the client being interviewed will want to talk about her partner and will resist discussing herself. After the first interview (and even in this) the counsellor must aim at talking with the client about the client's own feelings and ideas, and whenever possible lead back the discussion to the client and away from the partner. In this way a more professional relationship will be created, in which the client can be led to realize that the counsellor regards him as important for himself and not merely as a channel of information about the marriage. His opinions about his wife will also be regarded with reserve and his attempts to express them should be restricted.

Despite all the generalization which is inevitable in theoretical discussion, it must always be kept in mind that every client is a unique personality, as also is every counsellor, and their coming together forms a unique partnership. One of the exciting aspects of counselling is precisely this sense of a fresh adventure in each client who comes, and the certainty of a new angle on perhaps similar problems.

The creation of a helping relationship between counsellor and client depends upon the way in which the counsellor handles the discussion. Words are clearly the main tool, and in the interview situation he must use them to communicate a considerable range and depth of intuition, emotion, and empathy. He must be very careful to avoid jargon, however clever it may sound, and he must be certain that what he says is being understood in the sense in which he means it, and not in some other, perhaps more literal sense. He must also be careful to temper his vocabulary to the level of understanding of the client. It is always dangerous to use metaphor and analogy, especially of a flowery kind.

It will be seen that the interview is the central pivot of the whole process of counselling, during which the client must be enabled to express his hopes and fears, his fantasies and his difficulties, both real and imaginary. The counsellor must do his best to penetrate the mere words to the feelings behind them which cannot be expressed easily or clearly. There are, of course, other indications which emerge during interview—emotional outbursts, tears, anger, movement, which will also convey much of the client's feeling, but words are in most cases the important vehicle of communication.

In spite of its importance, interviewing is a process which seldom has enough attention paid to it in its own right. There are obviously many different kinds of interview, from that between employer and prospective employee to the interview between psychotherapeutic worker and client. In some cases, insufficient thought is given to the preparation of the setting. Even in many professional settings, there is no apparent attempt to create an atmosphere in which the client feels at home. There is often a barrier, such as a desk, between the two people, and this can raise all kinds of feeling in the client. He will, if he is troubled by feelings of inferiority or of anger against authority, perhaps be taken back to the time when he stood before his headmaster for some misdemeanour, or recall the emotions he felt when interviewed by some other authority figure in his life. What he says may be conditioned by something as simple as this. Offices of legal and medical practitioners are frequently of a somewhat forbidding aspect, with the result that clients or patients fail to do themselves justice.

The setting in counselling should be informal, and aimed at allowing the client to be at ease as much as may be possible. Freedom from interruption should be regarded as a matter of primary importance. The client's reception in the counsellor's room, as well as in the outer office or waiting-room, should be as pleasant as can be managed.

Direction of possible angles of the conversation should be avoided. Opening remarks are always of special importance, and should be non-committal without being banal. It will usually be known that the client has come because of some marital problem, but before an opening interview the nature of the problem will not often have been revealed. Early talking should therefore be left as much as possible to the client. His appearance and attitude are important—whether he is cheerful naturally, or making some effort to appear so: if he is exceptionally dejected or trying to appear casual. The manner of dress and general appearance must be noticed: is the client an older woman trying to look young, for example? Such observation can tell the counsellor a great deal, and it is necessary to regard them as part of the interview.

A plan or "structure" of an interview is always something to be borne in mind, but it is vital in a first interview to allow it to proceed as naturally as possible, with the counsellor noting carefully how it develops. In this initial meeting, which may be the first of many, counsellor and client will be looking at each other and observing reactions. The client especially, usually anxious and perhaps uncertain of his reception, is trying to make some impression on the counsellor. Possibly he wants to enlist help or sympathy, possibly to convey his anger or depression, possibly he is searching for words and the means of useful communication. On his side, the counsellor faces the task of listening to what is said, assessing it in terms of deeper meaning, trying to see why the client uses the words he does and brings the particular images and examples. He looks for the needs expressed and unexpressed, and tries to interpret the feeling revealed and concealed. The first interview is often confused and difficult. The client must be given every chance to put forward what he wants to say, even if the counsellor finds it hard to see what significance it may have.

Subsequent interviews may be better planned, as the counsellor is able to select the topics which seem most to trouble the client, and tries to "work through" them according to his skill, ability, and perceptiveness. This involves looking behind the immediate difficulties and anxieties presented, and bringing into the open the feelings which lie behind them, often of a painful or frightening nature. The more the counsellor succeeds in allowing the client to express his feelings and fantasies, and is able to accept and understand them without condemnation, the more is real help and reassurance possible. This process contributes to the building-up of the essential relationship, which grows with the realization that the counsellor feels "with" the client, and is interested in his real anxieties. The two are then able to share in the experience of looking at the problems and conflicts which present themselves. The client is enabled to examine attitudes in different areas of his life and experience, and to realize that his feelings of goodness and badness or of confused ambivalence can be shown safely and even talked about with a person who cares. Often he is able to grow in maturity because he feels himself to be a more satisfactory, confident, and individual personality. This sharing process is one of the vital components of the counselling relationship.

The next question to be considered is that of control in counselling interviews, and is also of major importance. Forms of control of this nature will vary widely, and are not always easily discernible, since conscious and unconscious factors will influence the situation. In addition, there may be a struggle between the counsellor and the client for control, and this struggle is frequently, though not always, realized by both. Control may be assumed or surrendered during an interview, especially if the counsellor is sufficiently skilled to realize the ways in which he can helpfully use and interpret what is happening.

Normally it is unwise for the counsellor to take control of the interview situation to such an extent that he directs the client's thoughts and ideas. It is important that he allows the client to express his own feelings, but he must try to become aware of the significance of the ideas put forward, and of their relationship to the general pattern of the interview. He should discourage the client from putting forward merely opinions or entering into a diatribe, unless he intends to use these in some helpful way.

A client may attempt quite direct control of the interview—for example, by demanding some specific action by the counsellor. Similarly, the counsellor may take control by restricting the topics of discussion, or by imposing a time limit. Some forms of control may be helpful, but others equally may be harmful, perhaps raising anxiety rather than creating true reassurance.

Control on the level of the unconscious is clearly more difficult to perceive and assess. Nevertheless, it is a powerful force in an interview situation. Its existence must always be recognized even if its effects cannot be immediately appreciated.

To consider first of all a very common interview pattern, it often appears that if the client is to be allowed to express his feelings in a manner helpful to him, he will monopolize the whole discussion. Some people are so demanding of attention and time that they will go on talking all the time and so give the counsellor little opportunity to intervene. It is necessary at some point for the counsellor to show such clients that this is happening, and such intervention is one form of control. It should be undertaken by the use of interpretation—by looking at the demands made and their cause of motivation—and not by frequent or brusque interruption. Often such clients are to an extent aware of their excessive demands and consuming greed. Recognition of it by the counsellor without condemnation may itself provide an apparently disproportionate amount of relief. Furthermore, such recognition followed by control may be greatly needed by a client. He may unconsciously be seeking to be controlled because he feels guilt about the demands he is making, and the counsellor may be the first person who has understood this need.

A more subtle and less helpful form of control may arise when a counsellor is afraid of a particular area of discussion and tries to avoid it by some form of interruption, thus leading the client away from it. This may be difficult for the counsellor to admit, or even to perceive, but the possibility must be considered. Conversely, the counsellor may allow the discussion to move in channels in which he feels safe, or which are exciting to him. This also may be hard to recognize, since it may be an unconscious form of direction by the counsellor.

Interrupting the client either to question him or to interpret is another form of direct control. In early interviews such interruptions should be kept to a minimum, until the client understands the pattern of interview and some confidence has begun to exist. Otherwise, the thread of thought and feeling may be broken, and not easily, if ever, resumed in quite the same way.

Ideally, any form of control ought to be considered in terms of timing and effect. It has been suggested that when a client appears emotionally over-demanding, some interpretation should be given rather than an ill-considered interruption.

Such interpretation may lead to hostility, which may be

useful and can perhaps be taken up. But the question of the right moment to interpret the client's fantasies or behaviour is always one of difficulty, and will depend upon the way in which the client is able to put forward his "story", which will vary from the incoherent to the cold and logical narrative. It will depend also upon the state of mind in which the client is and upon the point the relationship has reached. Other factors will be the intelligence of the client and his emotional and physical condition.

One question which has to be faced is that of the amount of time which can be given to an interview, and this is also a form of control. An hour is a useful guide, and although this may be considered long when compared with a professional interview, counsellors may aim at this length of time. It ought not to be exceeded. The client should know how long the interview is to last, but there will be those who will try to prolong the discussion and thereby obtain a larger share of the counsellor's time. The gentle interpretation of excessive demand, again in terms of greed, may be helpful in this situation also. Sometimes this demand is made by the client raising an apparently important topic just as the allotted time expires, and even as the door is opened to let the client depart. The counsellor may suggest that the point is raised in a subsequent interview, and indeed, if it is a matter of real urgency, it will undoubtedly appear in some form at the next interview.

Finally, there is the question of terminating a case. This expression is sometimes inaccurate, since even where there seems to have been a definite conclusion, a client will return again and again for help of some kind. But in most cases there is a time when most of the useful work seems to have been accomplished. It is by no means always easy to decide when this point has been reached, or how to complete the relationship. With some very dependent clients, the termination may be interpreted by them as a serious rejection, even though they may have achieved a degree of maturity during counselling. Many others will themselves realize that they have been enabled to look at their problems to the extent that there is no need for further help at a certain point, and will indicate this in a fairly clear way. Definite lines for completing a case cannot be marked out, except that, broadly speaking, some preparation ought to be made—perhaps by lengthening intervals between meetings or by directly informing the client during an interview and assessing his reaction. Much will depend on the tolerance margin of the individual counsellor, the depth of the problems brought, and his ability to cope with them, as well as the time available, apart from the internal and external pressures upon him. The counsellor must judge for himself by learning and experience the client whose dependence is unlikely to be much altered and the client who, whilst needing a large number of interviews, will ultimately achieve a greater degree of maturity and adjustment in his relationships.

It may be felt that the form of interviewing outlined is an ideal to be aimed at but seldom achieved. We are well aware of the pressures of time and of emotion upon the counsellor, but at least these ideas may be borne in mind, and may provide some method where previously one was hardly considered. There can be no exact prescription for interviewing technique: within a general framework it is for each counsellor to work out his approach to this difficult art in his own individual way.

List of Recommended Books

Interviewing: Its Principles and Practice, Garrett, F.S.A. of America, New York, 1958.

A Modern Approach to Marriage Counselling, Herbert and Jarvis, Methuen, 1958.

Shared Phantasy in Marital Problems, Bannister and Pincus, Codicote Press, 1965.

Marital Tensions, Dicks, Routledge & Kegan Paul, 1967.

8. AREAS OF TREATMENT

We have tried to show that our approach to marital work is appropriate not only for marriage counsellors but also for all whose work involves them with people who have matrimonial problems. Those who are not counsellors may well prefer to avoid a counselling relationship of any great depth, perhaps doubting their skill or feeling that the situation may arouse feelings beyond their control. It is still, however, desirable that professional people meeting their fellows in time of such distress arising from family problems should be able not only to recognize the immediate causes of unhappiness but also to realize that these are related to underlying factors. They will then be in a position at least to offer a form of help superior to the giving of superficial advice.

We must add that those who wish to be able to do more than to recognize problems beneath the surface would be wise to submit themselves to a form of selection and training such as that offered by the National Marriage Guidance Council, since training is essential for those who are anxious to work with marital problems at any real depth. It is also necessary to obtain an independent opinion as to one's suitability for such work, since it is difficult to perceive one's own limitations.

Turning now to methods of helping, it is possible to distinguish three areas in which professional people of goodwill may be able to assist in marital problems which they encounter. A recognition of these areas will be helpful also to marriage counsellors in structuring their interviews and in looking at the material brought out in discussion.

In the first place, there are the largely practical and material circumstances which can be considered, and some attempt may be made to keep the interview within these bounds. It must be borne in mind that these "factual" elements are only the superficial aspects of the situation, masking the other dimensions. Secondly, it is possible to go on to consider the personality factors—for example, the degree of maturity or the emotional pattern—of each client. Thirdly, an attempt may be made to assess the relationship between these two sets of factors, and how they affect the way the clients behave towards one another. In this third area, one is combining facts with separate personality assessments and looking at the attitudes which result.

It is seldom that a client actually presents the situation in such simple terms: the extrication of the factual from the emotional, and the interrelation of all the factors uncovered, are part of the process of counselling. If this concept of areas of help is borne in mind, it is possible to recognize more clearly where assistance can best be given: or at what point further help cannot be given, when the client must either be referred to another person for more expert treatment or the contact terminated in the best way possible.

The first area, which we have loosely described as the factual, will include the material circumstances of the client. It should contain a consideration of early family life and the background of the parents: not so much in terms of searching out emotional relationships as in attempting to get some idea of concrete situations. It is important to bear in mind, however, that what appear to be incontestable facts may be tinged with fantasy. It is useful to know whether a client was brought up in a family with both parents living together, or in some other environment. The parental background, in its turn, is important: did either of the parents suffer any specific deprivations, material or physical? Were there any circumstances of poverty? It is vital also to learn the number of brothers and sisters, and the age gaps between them, as well as the position of the client in the family. These factors are important not only in themselves, but also later when we come to the second area of help, in assessing the feelings of the client which may arise from them.

Knowledge of the district in which the client was born is helpful in viewing the present situation: it may indicate whether or not the client feels he has moved up or down socially. The type of education received and the response to it are relevant topics. Social class is important, and differences in this between partners can create misunderstandings and tensions. What may seem a superficial clash over habits which the husband has always accepted as natural but which increasingly irritate the wife may be symptomatic of serious differences in each partner's identification with social mores. It is possible for the counsellor to intervene usefully in such a situation. Sometimes a fairly simple interpretation of the position may lead on to a helpful discussion. In other cases opportunity may be afforded to look in depth at why in fact one or other of the partners in the first place felt the need to marry out of his social class. But this is trespassing into the third area of help we have indicated.

Another factor in this part of the exploration is housing: not only of the partners themselves but also of their parents. To some extent this will tie up with some of the circumstances already mentioned. More simply, the practical as well as the emotional problems of a family which for example is living in very close proximity to other families, with little or no privacy, will affect the marital situation. Where there are several children sleeping in the same room as their parents, the normal enjoyment of sexual intercourse is likely to be frustrated. Even under less crowded conditions this may occur, adversely affecting the marriage relationship.

The difficulty young couples frequently have in obtaining a home of their own may not only lead to the setting up of a home with the parents, with all the attendant problems, but may also result in the working out of unconscious feelings about leaving home and parents. There is often much ambivalence over this, especially where there is unconscious dependence on a parental figure. Counsellors and social workers have ceased to be surprised that in many cases where the couple have been living with parents removal to a separate home does not solve their problems but increases them, because of a deep-seated inability to accept responsibility or to separate from parents. This is the classical situation of "I'm going back to mother".

Another consideration of the first importance in any marriage is that of the children. We are not here thinking of the ambivalent feelings brought into any union when there are children, or conversely when there is a refusal to allow a child to be conceived, but of the differing ways in which the children of the marriage may be regarded or used as weapons by their parents. Those whose work lies in the various courts are constantly having this factor forced upon their notice. The feelings of a mother especially when she is involved in a difficult marital situation are likely to be influenced by anxiety about the future of the children, and it is all too easy for a counsellor to play upon this and urge her to "keep the marriage going for the sake of the children". This is almost always bad counselling. The need for long and serious discussion in such cases is vital, and it is inadvisable to take short cuts of this kind despite the fact that the social and economic disadvantages of a separated mother may be considerable.

The presence of children, however important as a stabilizing element in a marriage, creates problems of a practical kind in terms of restricting the opportunity for the parents to go out together or even to be alone together. Some marriages reach their breaking point through factors of this kind.

Again, although the facts are necessarily highly interrelated with the emotions, the circumstances of the birth of the children should be studied. The possibility of painful or difficult birth, the attitude of the husband or even of the grandparents, can colour the ensuing years of marriage. The spacing and the number of the children, and whether they were "wanted", are also to be noted.

This sort of information may throw light on the physical health of the clients. A couple who have to struggle for existence because of the ill health of one partner may have confused feelings of affection, hatred, and guilt: perhaps of bitterness, but perhaps also of pride in maintaining a home at all: of fear and anxiety about the future, and what "they" (the authorities) are going to do about it all. There may be deep and complex emotions to be looked at, which will never emerge until the health factor is at least known.

The duration of the marriage and the ages of the husband and wife may well be affecting its course, and although it is not possible here to consider all the implications in detail, some will be obvious in very early interviews and can be borne in mind to use in later interviews even if they do not at once appear as problems. Considerable disparity in age, for example, may indicate need in the younger partner for a parent-figure or for security and this need should be explicitly explored. It may also reveal a need in the other partner for a dependent partner—an example of the unconscious collusion which we have previously mentioned.

Finally, we would mention the types of employment in which either partner is engaged, and the degree of satisfaction which each obtains from it. Over-absorption in, or unhappiness arising from, work may well contribute to marital problems. Sometimes these problems of employment show up in a different form—for example, where the husband refuses to allow his wife to go out to work when she wants to. Such situations are symptomatic of underlying needs which again should be explored.

These, then, are some of the areas which we have designated as being of a more factual or material nature, and we have tried to show how they may link up with deeper needs. Some people will feel that they must try to limit their efforts to these areas, and these would be well advised to refer the clients to someone of greater skill or training if there is need—as there usually will be—for further help.

The second possible area we have called the individual personality one. This work here will essentially mean putting into practice the ideas of therapeutic relationship which we have discussed, particularly in Chapters 3 and 4. As we have already indicated, those who are to be seriously concerned with marital problems should seek training, as only in this way is it possible to begin to recognize the important psychological concepts discussed here and to attempt to work with them.

There will, of course, be marriages in which mental illness is a dominating factor, and there is a great need for counsellors and their co-workers to have a working knowledge of the commoner symptoms of mental illnesses. They should have a ready access to medical and psychiatric consultation. It is true that enthusiasm and pertinacity on the part of those who are working for marital adjustment may enable some to carry quite severely disturbed clients, but it may also prevent those clients from receiving expert diagnosis and treatment. There should be no hesitation in seeking such expert help, and ideally it should be readily forthcoming.

Other more obvious problems will often arise in the course of the counselling which are apparently due to the personality of one partner. Alcoholism is a frequent source of marital difficulty. Here the counsellor may not only need to explore the possibility of treatment for the alcoholic, but perhaps more importantly try to resolve the anger and perhaps the guilt of the other partner. Indeed, the treatment of this spouse is perhaps more fruitful, since there may well be more hope of some fairly immediate alleviation and of a better future adjustment to the circumstances.

Much the same is true of drug addiction, and this may become an increasing problem in the future in view of the growing number of drug-dependent people. It should again be said that those who "select" a partner who already has some deviation or instability are seeking, unconsciously, to satisfy some emotion of their own. The more hopeful task of the counsellor is to try to look at this aspect and if possible to see what the need may be if it can be recognized or admitted.

In the experience of the writers, more marital unhappiness than is generally realized arises because of the homosexual pattern of one or other of the partners. This idea is often misunderstood. It does not mean that the individual is a practising homosexual, but that he or she has failed to work through the stage of adolescence in which these feelings are uppermost, and in consequence the sexual drive has not become properly focused on the opposite sex. This condition remains latent, the subject often not being aware of it, but in the intimacy of marriage, the underlying feeling can appear in the relationship in a variety of ways. Some cases of frigidity or impotence must be regarded as manifestations of this pattern. Even where there is no recognition of it, the counsellor may find that anxiety about the condition is present, and it will emerge after a number of interviews. This is another aspect of the emotional conflicts which people experience with regard to the masculine and feminine parts of their personalities, and the male and female roles they should play. Where both partners are undergoing such anxieties, they may well be involved in deep disturbances.

This leads naturally to the third area of help which was mentioned: that of relationship between the separate personalities making up the marriage. The ways in which each partner needs and uses the other is central to most marital problems. The peculiar intimacy of the marriage situation will reactivate many of the fantasies and feelings of early childhood and of subsequent developmental periods. The actual choice of a mate will be largely conditioned by unconscious emotional needs, and one of the major tasks of the trained counsellor is identifying and teasing out the emotional interdependence of the two individuals.

The emotional collusion may be quite unconscious, as already indicated in Chapter 3, although to the counsellor it may become apparent early in the interviews. It may, for example, produce a partnership in which there appears to be almost continual quarrelling and even violence, and yet the couple remain together because their relationship fulfils mutually some deep need: for conflict, for excitement, for sexual gratification—the possibilities are many.

This third area, then, is the product of the other two. The marriage relationship will be built up from the need of each partner for an object-person fitting in with his own loving and hating feelings: his emotional situation generally, his maturity, and his capacity to relate to others. It is the purpose of the counsellor to try to understand these needs, to look at their interplay within the marriage, and to look with one or both the partners at the effect on the marriage relationship.

List of Recommended Books

Human Growth and the Development of Personality, Kahn, 2nd edn., Pergamon, 1968.

Sexual Deviation, Storr, Pelican, 1964.

9. SPECIAL PROBLEMS

HAVING discussed the various methods and techniques of marriage counselling, we can now look at some situations in which there seems less likely to be a successful outcome in helping the marriage. There may be purely practical courses of action which suggest themselves, such as separation or divorce, and the counsellor may help the couple to part in a manner less painful than it might otherwise have been. He may, however, have to accept that he cannot help at all except in the very general sense of having been a good listener. This acceptance may be difficult, especially for someone who is accustomed to success in other spheres, but it happens quite occasionally, and this in itself may help the counsellor to feel less frustrated. There are many clients who can make any person who comes into contact with them feel useless, and who can turn anything normally good into something bad and depressing. The counsellor may try to interpret this back to the client, but he may not have much success.

There are other circumstances in which counselling is liable to fail. The client may have a basic lack of intelligence, and although this is not in itself a bar to helpful relationship, it may prevent the client from accepting the reality of the problems. There may be some physical or pathological abnormality, or mental illness in which reality does not seem to exist. In some cases of this kind the other partner may be helped, as he or she will frequently feel some guilt about the mental illness which may be relieved by counselling.

In some people there is an apparent inability to communicate or to accept communication from others. This may be susceptible to highly specialized psychiatric treatment, but can rarely be helped by counselling, in which communication is essential.

The vital place of personal relationships has been stressed, but there are some who can only make a shallow relationship. It may be that the level of maturity in one or other partner makes a change of attitude in the other necessary to hold the marriage together, but that this change does not materialize in spite of skilled counselling. Relationships never stand still, and whereas the original need of the first partner may have been exactly for a shallow and undemanding partnership, his growth in emotional maturity leads him to seek a much deeper and more adult one. It is of great importance to realize that alteration of attitude in one partner affects the interpersonal pattern of the whole marriage in some way or another—this is why it is often possible to work with one partner only and yet have a good deal of success in affecting the whole atmosphere of the marriage.

Occasionally a situation will arise which seems to be purely of a physical nature, and which will break up a marriage. In one case, the husband left his wife after she had undergone a hysterectomy because he said she had lost her femininity. She became very depressed, virtually accepting his verdict, and was unable to accept help from the counsellor, though referred to a medical specialist. Obviously there were very deep emotional undertones on both sides, but in the event nothing constructive could be done.

Many people seem to need to live with problems despite all possible discussion and even realization of them. They will rationalize their emotional difficulties, as in a case where a young wife complained of her husband's cruelty and of sexual perversion, and was given a series of interviews over a long period. Her husband refused to admit that there was anything wrong in the marriage at all. The wife eventually left with the two children. During the period she was away she somewhat altered her complaint, and said that she needed sexual relations, which he denied her. She then returned to him, and continued to keep in touch with the counsellor. She achieved a more settled approach to her marriage when she was able to rationalize the problem of their whole sexual life by saying that she did not want any further intercourse because she did not want any more children. This, and the occasional contact with the counsellor, which seems to give her superficial reassurance, appears to enable her to tolerate the marriage, but she constantly talks of divorce as inevitable. The counsellor has tried to take up many aspects of her problems, but without further success, and referral to a psychiatric clinic was no more successful. It seems that she has to preserve the marriage on an insecure basis because of the deep insecurity of her personality.

Social environment may also make for problems in counselling. Sometimes a wife will not be able to consider any attempt at problem-solving which involves action not fitting in with her social milieu, or the future of the children. Many in this situation realize that they are not able to accept the help that is offered to them, and there are cases in which the stress emerges in ways other than in marital problems—for example, by some form of nervous or physical breakdown.

There are obvious marital problems likely to arise because of lack of housing. Apart from the material lack, there are many who seem to be without the ability to take responsibility for running a house and paying bills and rent. In some families this reacts on the marriage relationship, and is often at the root of many intractable "problem family" situations. Whatever kind of help is offered it cannot be accepted because the total inadequacy is so great. This inadequacy is not always due to lack of intelligence or other ability, but sometimes to a massive emotional blockage which is difficult to remove.

In some areas, counsellors may be called upon to give help to immigrants in their marital problems. This will probably cause difficulties, partly because of the unfamiliar patterns of culture and marriage custom, to say nothing of the problems of differing language and race. Indeed, the patterns of habit, custom, and behaviour in immigrants are such that the situation is sometimes not susceptible to counselling methods of permissive and problem-solving kinds, and it may be that more directive methods are needed. It is probable that different counselling methods will be devised in consultation with immigrant counsellors.

Religious belief will sometimes prevent the real application of counselling methods. There are those who accept from their religious advisers, or themselves possess, the sincere belief that their unhappy marriage is a necessary state of their life, and that they must bear the suffering involved because it is the divine will. Yet they come seeking some sort of relief, and curiously in many cases are reluctant to go to their religious adviser. Clients in this category are not common, but when a counsellor is confronted with one of them, he may be in a quandary. He may well feel that he should not attempt to look at the needs underlying such belief, yet without doing so he can give no help. It is often true that the belief itself holds the client's personality together, and that without it he would be even more unhappy. Furthermore, the counsellor's own religious convictions, or lack of them, may get in the way despite all his efforts. Encouragement to seek spiritual counsel, which may not be so unyielding as the client thinks, is often the only possibility in such cases.

Another dilemma which sometimes confronts the counsellor is concerned with his basic function. He normally hopes to effect some improvement in the marital relationship, but sometimes, although this does not happen and a separation occurs, the husband or wife is anxious to continue the interviews. The situation may become a psychotherapeutic one, and the counsellor may rightly feel he is not qualified to sustain a relationship which may call for much skill and give him grave anxiety. On the other hand, it may be that the conflicts and problems associated with the separation are such that the counsellor can greatly help in dealing with them. It would seem that the ideal way of treating this situation is for the counsellor to keep the interviews as rigidly as possible to the marriage and the client's feelings about it and about the separation, and not to be led into accepting extreme demands on his (the counsellor's) emotions or his time, especially if such demands are leading to psychological depths in which he feels uncertain.

The problem situations mentioned in this chapter may be infrequently encountered, but are selected as being in our experience amongst the more difficult. They have been discussed partly because there is occasionally a feeling, especially with new marriage counsellors and social caseworkers, that there ought nearly always to be a successful outcome of their efforts resulting in a reconciliation or in a demonstrable improvement in relationships. It is a sign of experience and maturity in a counsellor to be able to accept that, despite all possible skilled help, there are those who cannot respond, and not to become depressed or over-anxious about this. It is also true that none of us is gifted with divine foresight or omnipotence, and it may be that even where there is no apparently hopeful result, some reassurance has been given, or some slight adjustment made, so that improvement has been effected of which we may never be aware.

Recommended Book

Boundaries of Casework, Goldberg (ed.), Association of P.S.W.s, 1956.

10. COMMUNITY HELP AND REFERRAL—I

One of the important factors in helping with family problems is the ability to assist clients to select and use to the fullest extent the various agencies and services provided by the community. In marital work especially, this covers a very wide field. During the course of a single case, referrals may be made to solicitors, perhaps through the Legal Aid Scheme; to the Children's Department; to the Department of Health and Social Security; to the Housing Department; to the Welfare Department; and to many other agencies. All these and others may be suggested to the client, who will require support and guidance whilst considering what action to take.

A wide knowledge of possible helping agencies may be vital in dealing with a marital case. Such facilities tend to be insufficiently used, or used in the wrong way. General practitioners, for example, will send a wife to a solicitor when a little knowledge would have suggested a probation officer or a marriage counsellor in the first instance. Indeed, with some knowledge of counselling on the part of the doctor she might have been given enough direct help not to need either. It is depressing to discover how many unhappy people have been passed from one agency to another without receiving the basic help they needed.

All agencies and individuals concerned in any way with families ought to be far more aware of the many ways in which help can be given in time of need, and so promote more intelligent co-operation and referral. In addition, the agencies and individuals would more easily understand the needs of each other's patients and clients.

Dr. Caplan of Harvard University has suggested useful concepts on methods of dealing with various types of crisis in families and individuals. He distinguishes between the need for preventing a crisis, intervention in it, and the necessity for the community to make the best use of its means to cope with the recurrent crises of human existence.

This would involve all those engaged in the work of helping, from whatever angle, getting together to obtain far more knowledge of each other not only as workers but also as individuals. Such meeting together is of immense value: how much easier it is to ask aid from someone whom one knows personally than from some anonymous departmental telephone voice. All social workers and counsellors should get to know their communities, and not be office-bound and impersonal. At present, it seems probable that the use of community resources is the least realized tool of those who work with people.

On the other hand, it must also be understood that the use of others should be seen not as "passing the buck" but as referral for more skilled or appropriate help; that there is some specialist necessity in the referral.

With these thoughts in mind, let us look at some of the principal people and agencies to which and from which wives and husbands with problems tend to be referred. Since the family doctor, through the respect in which his profession is held, and his contact with families in times of extreme stress, is often the first person to be consulted, it seems appropriate to talk first about him.

General practitioners in medicine are usually busy and hard-pressed people. For this reason they are unlikely to have time to explore underlying factors, although they may suspect them in patients who are in matrimonial difficulty. Moreover, they are not generally skilled in the recognition of the need of patients in this field, and will tend to treat physical symptoms without becoming involved in the emotional problems. There may well be wisdom in this, since involvement of the doctor in marital cases could place him in the position of an arbiter between husband and wife, or even of a witness in court, which might destroy his relationship with the patient.

But if the doctor has sufficient skill and perception just to recognize the problems, he may be able to do something effective himself in looking at them with his patient. Dr. Balint has shown how investment of this sort saves a great deal of work at a later stage. If the doctor knows enough about other agencies, he can safely refer the patient elsewhere.

By reason of the long and honourable tradition of medicine, the medical practitioner is accepted as a highly skilled and professional person. He could be of immense importance in detecting the need for marital work at an early stage. General practitioners should be given every opportunity, by special courses, by experiments in consultation and team-work with skilled lay or medical counsellors, or by other suitable means, to develop perceptiveness and to learn how to intervene most effectively.

Referral of marital cases to medical practitioners is normally indicated where breakdown of a physical or mental nature is feared.

Although there is frequently a request from a client that the wife or husband should be seen by a psychiatrist, such referral will in many cases be a misuse of the time of a highly specialized practitioner. Psychiatrists have to some extent become the victims of popular propaganda, and are often regarded as capable of performing some magical and speedy operation on their patients, after which all will be well. In fact, the psychiatrist is basically a specialist in mental illness. He may be a consultant, and so very selective in undertaking treatment. Again, he may treat his patients by some form of psychotherapy or analysis, although at the present time it appears that treatment is mainly by drugs or some physical means.

It is possible, therefore, that direct referral to a psychiatrist of clients who are emotionally disturbed, or (from his specialized standpoint) mildly neurotic, is unrealistic. It is advisable to be as certain as possible that the client has problems which, in this dimension, are appropriate to the particular service to which he is referred. There may be difficulty over those diagnosed as psychopaths, since the problems they present often appear mainly in the form of inability to accept normal social living. In our experience many psychiatrists feel that such people cannot be usefully treated, although some, such as Dr. Maxwell Jones, have had some success in this difficult area.

Some general hospitals now have units for the special

treatment of psychiatric patients, and use is made of these to avoid unnecessary admissions to the specialized hospitals. In these units also, pressure is very great, and their first duty is to the mentally ill. Reference to such a unit can result in help being given in marital cases, perhaps by the psychiatric social worker in consultation with the psychiatrist.

Some hospitals have their own units for assisting marital and family problems in a direct way. The Tavistock Institute for many years carried out this work through the Family Discussion Bureau (now the Institute of Marital Studies), where treatment is undertaken as well as invaluable work in research and training. The Cassel Hospital at Ham Common in Surrey not only assists married couples with treatment, but also trains medical and social workers in this field of work.

Psychoanalysis in any form may be of help to a couple in matrimonial difficulties, but is normally very expensive, and the number of analysts is small, so that the possibility of referral to an analyst is not hopeful. Similarly, forms of psychotherapy by trained psychotherapists are not widely available, although in the future there may be much development in this direction in ways not yet realized. In any event, psychoanalysis and formal psychotherapy are directed to the individual, and application of these methods to the interplay of feeling in marriage may be difficult to achieve.

Turning from the possibilities of medical referral, it is often assumed that the clergy are suitable people to deal with marital problems. This is partly because of the involvement of the Church in marriage, and partly because some people would naturally turn to a priest in time of trouble. Clearly, the responsibility of the parish priest for the well-being of his parishioners is well established. In recent times this idea of consulting the parish priest has perhaps become less common. Those clergy of any denomination who are able to help in the skilled way we have been discussing appear to be limited in number, although the churches generally are becoming much more aware of the need for deeper understanding of marital problems. Some clergy are turning to the National Marriage Guidance Council for help by referral or for training, and the Roman Catholic Church has its own Marriage Advisory

Council. Marital and family work would certainly appear to be an area in which the churches could effectively involve themselves with the lives of ordinary people. Unfair as it may be to many devoted priests, the man in the street at present is apt to feel that if he approaches a clergyman for help in matrimonial trouble, he will receive advice, exhortation, or (to him) somewhat unrealistic suggestions, rather than what he would regard as real help.

Solicitors and barristers are obviously very much concerned with marital problems in their clients, although their contact is usually more formal and limited to legal issues. Even in this situation, more consideration might sometimes be given to the non-legal problems of their clients. Lawyers might perhaps more frequently refer people to a marriage counselling agency in order to get a clearer view of their needs and more idea as to where their real problems may lie.

There are a number of agencies supported by the central government or local authorities which frequently receive requests for help. The probation service has a statutory duty to assist in the reconciliation of married couples, and a growing number of its officers receive special training in this work. In most cases, application for such help can be made direct to the probation officer, and although many clients come on their own initiative, referrals are made to the probation service by all agencies. Professional people such as doctors, solicitors, and clergy use this service quite commonly. It is unfortunate that the skilled help which the probation service can give may sometimes not be accepted because of its association with courts and criminals, although, as has been said earlier, to some people the underlying reason they come to this agency may be because they feel the need for an authority figure. Incidentally, this counselling function of the probation service is also available in the divorce courts, where probation officers act as welfare officers, although their primary duty is to make investigations concerning the welfare of the children in cases before the court.

It is often useful to refer to the probation officer cases in which there is a likelihood of court action, since he is in a position not only to attempt counselling, but also to help with legal referral where the client wishes this. He is also in touch with a wide range of agencies who may be able to help in a practical way. At least, he should be able to assist clients to look at their problems more clearly, and so enable them to come to a decision of their own volition, if they are capable of doing so. He should not press a client towards what he himself may consider the best course, although he will frequently, as part of the attempt to examine the problem together with the client, point out the likely consequences of any intended action.

The extension of legal aid to matrimonial cases has probably reduced the number of marital problems directly assisted by the probation service on a long-term basis. In terms of the general social well-being of the community this may possibly be retrograde. It is not often realized that occasionally a husband and wife who have obtained a legal separation, or a divorce, will become reconciled, and in such cases it is essential to have the help of a counselling service so that the problems causing the original separation can be discussed in the light of the reconciliation. In this way, the reconciliation may be made more lasting by a better understanding of its causes.

List of Recommended Books

The Probation Service, King (ed.), Butterworths, 2nd edn., 1966.
A New Look at Social Medicine, Anderson, Pitman Medical, 1965.
Social Casework in a General Medical Practice, Collins, Pitman Medical, 1967.
The Provision of Treatment for Disturbed Adolescents, London Boroughs (private), 1968.
The Doctor, His Patient, and the Illness, Balint, Pitman Medical, 1957.
Psychotherapeutic Techniques in Medicine, Balint, Tavistock, 1965.
Social Casework for the State, Pollard, Pall Mall, 1962.
Social Casework: Principles and Practice, Timms, Routledge & Kegan Paul, 1964.
An Approach to Community Mental Health, Caplan, Tavistock, 1961.
Principles of Preventive Psychiatry, Caplan, Tavistock, 1964.
Social Psychiatry, Maxwell Jones, Pelican, 1968.

11. COMMUNITY HELP AND REFERRAL—II

THERE are numerous other agencies which are liable to be forced into awareness of marital problems by becoming the recipients of the worries of their clients. An obvious example is the Health Visiting Service. Although its traditional concern has always been with mothers and young children, its role is increasingly the first line of defence in preserving the total health of the family, and this also makes it the first line of attack on family problems. The training of the health visitor in medical fields, and her close involvement with the medical profession, may enhance her attraction as a person with whom to discuss confidential and perplexing problems, which indicate tensions and ills in the family. Since these are not likely to be altered radically by the practical skills, it is important that the health visitor should know when her client is uttering a "cry for help" on the psychological level. Only in this way can the needs of the client be met by timely referral to an appropriate specialist agency, which can look at the difficulties before they become intractable, and may provide a counselling service if necessary.

Health visitors are not yet equipped to give the type of counselling which we have described, but many who have received the more recent type of training could expand and deepen their work with guidance from the skilled counsellor. Those responsible for this training now realize that the duties of the health visitor cannot be restricted to the giving of medical advice, since clients will often make demands of quite a different nature, though equally important.

The Children's Department of a local authority is another agency with an influential part to play in family adjustment. The emphasis of the Children Acts of 1963–9 on maintaining children in their own homes demands much more than the meeting of material needs. Training in a skilled approach to marital problems would seem to be a vital necessity for child care officers and for those who work in the residential services of the Children's Department, particularly if we hold the view that the roots of juvenile adjustment to life lie in the relationships which are begun, developed, and sustained within the family group, especially between child and parent.

In the many cases encountered by workers with deprived children the chances of damaged personality are considerable, as there are neither parents nor good parental figures. Where parents (or parent-substitutes) can be assisted in adjusting sufficiently to become "good figures" for their children, there is an obligation to train the staffs of Children's Departments in working towards such adjustment in the way we have described. Taking a long view, this would seem to be in the best interests of the children.

This would mean that those who work with children would be able to recognize swiftly the marital problems in the families concerned, and would be prepared to look at the difficulties not only of the children but also of the marriage with which they have to live and share the tensions. Child care work, it is increasingly realized, does not mean working with the child alone, or even working mainly to improve the material conditions of the environment, but demands an understanding of the deeper relationships within the family group. Even now, however, the potential capacity of child care work in this sphere is imperfectly understood.

The possibilities of the sharing of marital cases between social workers with children and other social workers or marriage counsellors are very considerable. In some districts it is quite a frequent occurrence for a child care officer to work with the children in a family in which a worker from another social agency is counselling the parents. This may be a useful situation for many reasons, emotional and material, although clearly it demands close co-operation between all concerned, as well as a definite understanding of the role played by each.

Education welfare officers are often placed in a situation

where they must appreciate that parental difficulties are causing children to stay away from school. Some cases of this kind are now known to be due to school-phobia, or school-refusal. This is basically the disinclination, or even inability, of a child to leave home and attend school because of anxiety about tensions within the family, usually between the parents. Since this condition is not infrequently misunderstood, an example will help to make it clearer.

This case concerned a boy of 14 who absented himself from school on many occasions and for long periods also. He was an intelligent boy, good at school work when he attended, and reasonably popular with the other boys, although he did not make friends easily. The parents were also intelligent, both worked regularly, and there was no real shortage of money, though there were frequent financial crises owing to mismanagement. Father was a somewhat withdrawn personality given to violent outbursts of temper, and most of the time leaving responsibility to his wife. She was a vivid personality, who was subject to frequent violent outbursts, and dramatized herself much of the time. There was a state of permanent tension, broken by quarrels involving physical assaults and threats of separation. The other children reacted by withdrawing from the situation, going out or staying in their room, but this boy developed a state of great anxiety which stemmed from insecurity. He was much attached to his mother, and afraid to go to school in case he returned home to find she had carried out her threat to leave home. So great was his distress that he developed physical symptoms of sickness and other ailments, so that he was able to produce certificates from his doctor on several occasions to cover his absences. The education welfare officer dealing with the case did so in close co-operation with a social worker who was counselling the parents. Although the school attendance was always poor, it improved slightly, and the boy on leaving school became more settled, undoubtedly partly because the counselling had by that time had some effect and the home situation was slightly more secure. If the issue had been forced, and legal proceedings perhaps instituted, the boy's future would have been jeopardized, and such was the position between the parents that the home could easily have been broken up, with much worse results for the other children also.

Education welfare officers should receive some training to help them to recognize emotional problems. It might be argued that they should be able to attempt counselling work also, but it may be sufficient that recognition of deeper problems should lead to referral to a counselling agency and co-operation with it.

Parents who have problems arising with children are often sent for help to the Child Guidance Clinic, and those clinics which have sufficient staff available spend much of their time in looking at the marital problems of parents. Such clinics are well equipped for this purpose, consisting as many do of a psychiatrist, psychiatric social worker and psychotherapist, with the close co-operation of an educational psychologist who may have joint responsibility for the professional methods adopted in the clinic.

Since the effect of marital relationships on the children of a marriage has been mentioned, it is appropriate to suggest that there ought to be much greater awareness within schools of the problems involved. It is possible that the development of a school counselling service will help in this, but it seems also that training colleges for teachers should pay far more attention to this vital aspect in the lives of children. The subject of family background often appears to be neglected in favour of more academic training. In discussions with students one is often surprised and disappointed to discover a lack of understanding about family problems. At the very least, it would seem desirable for teachers to know the local agencies and their functions, so that they may through the head teacher or appropriate other channel refer usefully problems seen in their pupils perhaps having their origin in disharmony between parents which has reached a serious stage.

Local authority Welfare Departments deal mainly with the homeless, the aged, and the physically handicapped, but their officers will often come across cases of marital problems which they can refer to counselling agencies for this special kind of help. Much the same is true of mental welfare officers, although the marital problems confronting them may often appear insoluble because of the complications of severe mental illness. Nevertheless, occasionally the other partner of such a marriage may be helped more than at first might be thought possible.

Other official agencies such as the Department of Health and Social Security are in a position to refer cases of marital difficulties to skilled counsellors, as are personnel managers and welfare officers in industry. They should be able to recognize the indications for need of such help.

Outside the more official helping services already described, the best-known agency for marital work is the National Marriage Guidance Council, whose activities extend to all parts of the country. It has highly efficient selection and training procedure, and its trained counsellors (who are mainly voluntary) are able to deal with difficult marriage problems, helped if necessary by professional consultants. In many areas local marriage guidance councils have sufficiently proved their worth for the chief problem to be the existence of a waiting-list of clients seeking their help. Roman Catholics have their own council.

It is not always realized that the Family Planning Association has, in many areas, a marriage problems advisory service, chiefly concerned with cases of frigidity and sub-fertility, and able to accept referrals from other agencies. This Association is a very useful agency to which to refer sexual problems generally in marriage, and often works closely with local marriage guidance councils.

Citizens' Advice Bureaux do not provide a direct counselling service, but they may be of use in giving information about the location of social and counselling agencies in their district.

Most of this present discussion has necessarily been concerned with the treatment of marital difficulties which have already made themselves apparent. The preventive aspect, which is also of crucial importance, is met in the educational work undertaken by the National Marriage Guidance Council, as well as by some local education authorities. This work includes preparation for marriage courses, and the leading of group discussions in schools and youth clubs on relationships between the sexes.

In the long term, the co-operation of all agencies and people concerned with the social and individual welfare and happiness of those seeking their help is essential. If this co-operation is to achieve maximum effect, these agencies and workers must operate from common basic concepts. They will then realize that the varying problems with which they try to cope usually have their roots in the same deeper anxieties and conflicts to which all human beings are heir. The doctor seeing his patient may understand that the sickness he observes can sometimes be a symptom of needs which under different pressures might have emerged as delinquency or marital stress. The lawyer advising his client who is trying his patience by frequent changes of instructions may perhaps appreciate that this does not necessarily arise from stupidity, but from a need for attention or, more deeply, from a confusion the client feels about his marriage. Attempts to recognize and to understand the underlying problems of those who seek help will lead to greater clarity of discussion and the more effective meeting of the real needs.

List of Recommended Books

Guide to the Social Services, F.W.A., 1968.
Hall's Social Services of England and Wales (ed. Forder), Routledge & Kegan Paul, 1969.
A New Look at Social Work, Collins, Pitman Medical, 1967.
Fatherless Families, Wynn, Joseph, 1964.
An Anatomy of Social Welfare Services, Jeffreys, Joseph, 1966.
Unwillingly to School, Kahn and Neuster, Pergamon, 1967.

RECOMMENDED BOOKS FOR FURTHER READING

THERE is a considerable number of books on the various subjects allied to marriage counselling, but not many which are directly concerned with it. Furthermore, of those which have such direct bearing, several are more suitable for the serious student who desires an introduction to the deeper aspects which are allied to social casework and its techniques, which border on psychotherapy.

The books mentioned at the end of each chapter are those which have some bearing on the subject of that chapter, but the following list includes those for further reading by the more serious student. Some of them have already been included in the appropriate chapters.

Marital Tensions, Dicks, Routledge & Kegan Paul, 1967.

Social Casework in Marital Problems, Family Discussion Bureau, Tavistock, 1955.

Marriage, Pincus and others, Methuen, 1960.

A Modern Approach to Marriage Counselling, Herbert and Jarvis, Methuen, 1958.

Marital Breakdown, Dominian, Pelican, 1968.

Marriage Guidance, Wallis, Routledge & Kegan Paul, 1968.

Shared Phantasy in Marital Problems, Bannister and Pincus, Codicote Press, 1965.

Human Growth and the Development of Personality, Kahn, 2nd edn., Pergamon, 1968.

Social Casework: Principles and Practice, Timms, Routledge & Kegan Paul, 1964.

The Casework Relationship, Biestek, Allen & Unwin, 1961.

The Boundaries of Casework, Goldberg (ed.), Association of P.S.W.s, 1956.

Psychoanalysis Observed, Ryecroft (ed.), Pelican, 1968.

Childhood and Society, Erikson, Pelican, 1969.

The Child, the Family, and the Outside World, Winnicott, Pelican, 1967.

Sex and Society, Fletcher and Walker, Pelican, 1968.

Individual Morality, Hemming, Nelson, 1967.

INDEX

Acceptance 24, 35, 36, 39
Adolescence 11, 22
Adulthood 11
Advice 28, 29, 34, 67
Affection 35, 54
Aggression 10, 19, 24, 25, 26
Alcoholism 56
Ambivalence 25
Anger 14, 35, 45, 46
Anxieties 37, 46
Anxiety 38, 47, 54, 71
Attitudes 18, 19, 22, 31
Authority figure 24, 25

Badness 16, 19, 30, 36
BALINT, DR. M. 64
Barrister 67
BOWLBY, DR. JOHN 10

CAPLAN, DR. GERALD 70
Cassel Hospital 66
Catholic Marriage Advisory Council 66, 67
Child care officer 43, 70
Child Guidance Clinic 71
Children 4, 54, 70
Children and Young Persons Acts 69
Children's Department 63, 69, 70
Citizens' Advice Bureaux 73
Clarification 24, 29
Clergy 6, 33, 66, 67
Collusion 57
Colour 22
Concern 24
Condemnation 23, 24, 46, 48
Contraceptive 20
Criticism 23

Demandingness 10, 48
Dependence 49, 50
Depression 46
Deprived children 70
Destructive feelings 26
DICKS, DR. HENRY 42
Divorce 2, 33, 58, 68
Domination 9, 16
Drug dependence 56

Education welfare officer 70, 71, 72
Emotional immaturity 9, 15, 17, 26
Emotional maturity 9 f., 15, 17, 27, 47
Emotional stability 17
Extended family 2

Family 2, 5, 18
Family Planning Association 73
Fantasy 2, 4, 38, 44, 46, 49, 52, 57
Father 18
Fear 9, 38, 44, 54
Female role 17, 18, 57
Frigidity 56, 73

Greed 48, 49
Guilt 9, 15, 38, 41, 42, 48, 54

Hate 14, 25, 28, 38, 39, 54, 57
Hate-object 12

Health and Social Security, Department of 63, 73
Health visitor 69
Homosexuality 56
Hostility 14, 24, 25, 26, 37, 38, 48
Housekeeping money 28
Housing 53
Housing Department 63
Husband 3, 18, 35, 41, 42

Identification 18
Immigrants 4, 60
Impotence 56
Inadequacy 60
Industrial revolution 5
Infancy 11, 15
Infantile fantasies 19
Inferiority 20
Insight 31, 41
Institute of Marital Studies 66
Interpretation 31, 38, 48, 49
Interview
  control of 24, 47, 48
  direction of 45, 48
  first 46
  opening remarks 45

Jealousy 9, 31
JONES, DR. MAXWELL 65

Latey Committee 4
Legal aid 63, 68
Love 10, 14, 15, 16, 38, 39, 57
Love-object 11

Male role 18, 57
Maternal deprivation 10
Maternal role 17
MEAD, MARGARET 5
Medical practitioner 6, 33, 34, 45, 63, 64, 65
Mental welfare officer 72
Mother 15, 18, 30

National Marriage Guidance Council 6, 22, 23, 51, 66, 73
Needs 37, 46
Nuclear family 2

"Of Human Life" 3

Parent 10, 52
Parental figure 18
Paternal attitude 17
Personality 12, 14
Personnel manager 73
POPE PAUL VI 3
Possessiveness 15
Prejudices 23, 24, 37
Probation officer 33, 34, 43, 63, 67
Probation service 67
Projection 18
Psychiatric social worker 66, 72
Psychiatrist 65, 66, 72
Psychoanalysis 18, 28, 65, 66
Psychologist 72
Psychopath 65
Psychotherapy 18, 28, 61, 65, 66

Race 22
Reassurance 2, 8, 39, 46, 60, 62
Referral 32, 34, 41, 64
Rejection 20, 38
Relationship 8 f., 22, 25, 46
Religion 3, 22, 60, 61
Reparation 16, 42
Role
  female 17, 18, 57
  male 18, 57
  maternal 17
  playing 29, 30
  sexual 18

School counselling 72
School phobia 71
Security 35, 38
Seebohm Report 6, 43

Sexual intercourse 17, 19, 20, 42, 59
Sexual satisfaction 2
Social class 22, 53
Social workers 53
Solicitor 33, 63, 67
Spiritual counsel 61
Sub-fertility 73
Submission 9, 16

Tavistock Institute 66
Teachers 72
Training 51
Transference 25
Treatment 32

Unconscious collusion 16
Unconscious mind 14, 23
Unconscious motivation 30
Unconscious needs 57

Violence 35, 41, 42, 57

Welfare Department 63, 72
Welfare officer 73